A Trekking Guide to Dhaulagiri

Dhaulagiri Sanctuary
Dhaulagiri Circuit, Dhaulagiri Dolpo
Dhaulagiri Kopra Panorama
Gurja Himal

Siân Pritchard-Jones and Bob Gibbons

© Siân Pritchard-Jones and Bob Gibbons and Himalayan Map House, 2018

All rights reserved. No part of this publication may be reproduced or transmitted in any form or by any means without the prior written permission of the copyright holders.

ISBN: 9781986754040
First edition 2018

Text: Siân Pritchard-Jones and Bob Gibbons
Photos: Siân Pritchard-Jones and Bob Gibbons except where credited
Concept: Pawan Shakya (www.himalayanmaphouse.com)
Design: Santosh Maharjan
Maps: Nirjan Maharjan, Shree Krishna Maharjan

Front cover: Dhaulagiri from Rayakhor
Back cover: Dhaulagiri sunrise from Phedi
Title page: Dhaulagiri from Chitre

A Trekking Guide to
Dhaulagiri

Dhaulagiri Sanctuary
Dhaulagiri Circuit, Dhaulagiri Dolpo
Dhaulagiri Kopra Panorama
Gurja Himal

Siân Pritchard-Jones and Bob Gibbons

Highlights

Misty dawn on Dhaulagiri

Dhaulagiri from below Rayakhor

Dhaulagiri above Lete

Dhaulagiri from Kopra Ridge

Dhaulagiri South Face from Base Camp
(photo: Durba Paija)

Dhaulagiri, Tukuche Peak & Dhampus pass (right)
(view taken from Lubra pass)

Jirbang & Manapati ridge

Annapurna I, Fang and Annapurna South from Kopra

Cultural highlights

Two shrines at Bandi Ghat near Dhar

Porters pass a Shiva shrine near Pakhapani

Hanuman temple near Tatopani

Buddhist Chortens at Chharka, Dolpo

Jhi village at sunrise

Magar house in Ghyasikharka

Chimkhola village view

Gurjakhani village (photo: Joy & Duane Poppe)

On the trails

Off to school in Rayakhor

Rhododendrons are encountered in spring

Eerie cloud forest

Duitakholsa meadow

New trail near Odar (photo: Sanjib Gurung)

The 'exciting' Dragon Cliff

Dhaulagiri from snowy Kopra

Trail along the Kali Gandaki to Dana

Tilicho Peak, Annapurna I from Bhima Lojun pass, Dhaulagiri Dolpo Trek

Dhaulagiri from Duitakholsa meadow

Meeting the people

Curious child looking at the foreigners

Local farmer's wife

Magar ladies in Darmija

A woman's work is never done!

Who goes there!

Durba Paija in the Dhaulagiri Sanctuary

Local belles (photo: Sanjib Gurung)

The crew in Chhari: Sanjib, Dev, Samraj & Bishnu

Meeting the bullocks as well

And with luck, the Himalayan Tahr

Acknowledgements

Thanks to Udyog R Singh, Pawan Shakya, Dr D R Kafley and all the team at Himalayan Travel Guides / Himalayan Map House. Special thanks to Rajesh Sakya and the Myagdi Chamber of Commerce in Beni. In Jhi thanks to Dek Bahadur Magar, in Chhari to Bhakti Prasad Chyantal and in Chimkhola to Durba Paija – the Mistri or construction fixer for the new trail above Phedi – also for his superb pictures taken above Odar around Base Camp during a couple of construction trips. Thanks to Surendra Rana for his information.

Special thanks to Sanjib Gurung, Bishnu the cook, Samraj and Dev, our gallant porters. Many thanks to trek leader Ade Summers and Roland Hunter of The Mountain Company, who regularly run Dhaulagiri Circuit treks
(www.themountaincompany.co.uk)

Thanks as ever to top naturalist Rajendra Suwal for his section on the birds and natural history. Many thanks to old Himalayan hand Kev Reynolds, Cicerone author, who inspired us to go further on our journey to guidebook writing, and who has also trekked across most of Nepal. Also to Joy and Duane Poppe for the information and pictures of Gurja Himal (www.offthebeatentreks.org)

Huge thanks to Uttam Phuyal and all the staff at Hotel Moonlight – our home away from home – for the essential hot showers and good food at the end of the trek. Also to Sohan Shrestha at Pilgrims Hotel, and to Sitaram Bhandari, David Durkan, Ian Wall, Paulo Grobel and Bill Crozier. Thanks to Mingmar Sherpa of The Everest Equipment Shop for the great sleeping bags and jackets, still keeping us warm after thirteen treks.

For keeping us going, thanks to Dr Martin Ridley and Dr Yann Hurry. Also over the years thanks to Ravi Chandra, Mr Dhir, Jitendra Jhakri Tarali Magar and Jag Budha Magar, Kul Bahadur Gurung, Purna Thapa Magar, Rajendra B. Lama, Sanjib Gurung, Chhewang Lama and all their guides and porters. Every one of them has been a vital part of the trekking experience.

And finally, thanks to the reader, who can help to keep this book updated.

Please send your suggestions and updates to sianpj@hotmail.com, www.expeditionworld.com

The authors are particularly indebted to Sanjib Gurung, Ade Summers and Roland Hunter for their contributions.

Sanjib Gurung
Our ever-patient, enthusiastic mountaineering guide from the Makalu region, Sanjib is at the forefront of developing new trekking trails. Born in the small, isolated village of Mangsima, below the towering Tinjure Milke Danda ridge, he is one of ten siblings. His education was initially in Mangsima, but for further schooling and studies he had to go to Khandbari. He studied management but soon found that his passion was mountaineering, trek guiding, mountain biking and photography. He has undertaken a series of training programmes, speaks excellent English and lives in Kathmandu near Balaju with his wife. People like Sanjib are Nepal tourism's greatest assets: motivated, energetic and eager to promote his own region as well as other areas of Nepal. www.climbinghimalaya.com

Sanjib at Phedi

Ade Summers

Ade Summers first went to Nepal in 1996. He has trekked, explored and led many groups in the Himalaya ever since. Originally from South Wales in the UK, he has spent eight years in Australia. Before becoming one of the most experienced trek leaders on high altitude routes, he was a computer geek. Other guiding activities include mountain biking in Mongolia and Burma, sea-kayaking in Sydney and canyoning. He was also a lifeguard on Barry Island. When not on the trails of the Himalaya, the Karakoram, the Pamirs or other mountain regions, he can be found negotiating the treacherous slope of the staircase to Sam's Bar in Thamel, Kathmandu. (www.adetnw.com)

Advice to readers

We have done our best to ensure the accuracy of this guidebook as it goes to print. However, changes can and will occur during its lifetime. We advise you to check information about such things as transport, accommodation and food locally. Landslides and local politics may also change routes over time.

Magnificent panorama of Dhaulagiri, the Ruwachaur ridge (left) and Tukuche Peak (right)

The greater danger for most of us is not that our aim is too high and we miss it, but that it is too low and we reach it.
Michelangelo

www.yetiairlines.com

Warning
Please remember that walking in remote, high mountain areas is potentially dangerous. The publisher and authors have taken every care in producing this guide, but readers must take ultimate responsibility for themselves. Trail and weather conditions can change suddenly and readers must understand these natural risks. Trails in the Himalaya are sometimes exposed and narrow, and unsuitable for anyone who does not have a good head for heights. Those who are unsure or inexperienced should relish the additional safety of employing a fully trained and experienced Nepalese trekking guide.

Neither Himalayan Map House nor the authors can accept liability for damage of any nature (including damage to property, personal injury or death) arising from the information in this book, directly or indirectly.

Although there are now some local mobile phone networks throughout most (but definitely not all) of the trekking routes, foreign mobile phones may not work. Local people may be able to help and call a helicopter if necessary, but this will be expensive.

There are more health posts in the popular trekking regions than across most of Nepal, but that does not mean many. Apart from the marijuana growing freely alongside some of the trails, drugs are not available everywhere on most routes. Take a supply of all the medicines you are likely to use, as well as those you do not expect to need! Beware of yak and mules on the crowded trails. Always be prepared to help yourself in any eventuality. It may be the only way.

> It's a dangerous business, Frodo, going out your door. You step on to the road, and if you don't keep your feet, there's no knowing where you might be swept off to.
> ***The Lord of the Rings*, J R R Tolkien**

Earthquakes in Nepal: 2015

In April and May 2015 two powerful earthquakes struck Nepal, causing massive disruption to the country. Although many older houses and some historic temples were left in ruins across Kathmandu, the majority of buildings and infrastructure remained intact. Sadly the rural areas adjacent to the two quakes suffered more serious damage.

The main areas affected were below the peaks of Manaslu, Ganesh Himal, Langtang, Gauri Shankar and parts of the Everest region. However, despite all the earthquake damage, trekkers are already venturing into all the regions mentioned.

The Dhaulagiri region was spared the disastrous consequences. The entire Annapurna region, including Mustang and the Nar-Phu valley, was mostly unaffected. Trekking here is continuing as before, where lodges and dirt access roads remain in place to service trekkers' needs.

Further west, all of Dolpo, the Rara Lake area and the far western trails of Saipal and the Limi Valley also remain open for trekkers.

The Kanchenjunga and Makalu areas did not suffer any significant effects from the two quakes. The villages, lodges, trails, roads and hillsides were left intact; only a few isolated houses suffered.

Transport links between Kathmandu and the Terai, as well as along the main valleys of the region, remain open and functioning normally.

Some work has begun on rebuilding the historic heart of Kathmandu. It is to be hoped that the historic world heritage monuments, the amazing architectural wonders of the Kathmandu Valley, will once again be regenerated.

Earthquake Diaries: Nepal 2015

We were in Kathmandu during the month of May. Having become instant aid workers (buying up rice, tarpaulins, tin sheets and warm, locally made clothing using generous donations), we witnessed a remarkable few weeks in the country. After the first days of shock thousands of local people, young and old, engaged in the relief and rebuilding process with amazing energy. There is no doubt that the resilient people of Nepal will be back on their feet well ahead of expectations.

The country certainly needs the tourism sector to blossom again as soon as possible. Your trek will help this to happen more quickly.

Anyone wishing to know how 'amateur' aid works can read our *Earthquake Diaries: Nepal 2015*, published by Expedition World and available on Amazon websites worldwide, in colour, black & white and Kindle.

Contents

Preface	32
Introduction	34

BEFORE THE TREK — 40
Country background — 40
Geography	40
Climate	41
Natural history	42
Brief history	48
Religion and festivals	53
Cultural aspects	62
Helping the people	64

Practicalities — 67
Getting to Nepal	67
Visa information	69
Money matters	71

Trek planning — 74
Trek permits and TIMS	74
Maps	77
Budgeting	79
Style of trekking	80
Independent trekking	80
Fully supported group treks	83
Accommodation	86
Food	88
What to take	90

Staying healthy — 90
Altitude sickness & precautions	96
Mountain safety	97
Weather	98
Security	99

Kathmandu – gateway to the Himalaya — 100
Pokhara – after the trek — 105
Using this guide	107
Pre-trek checklist	109

THE TREKKING ROUTES — 111
Dhaulagiri Sanctuary Trek — 111
Dhaulagiri Sanctuary Plus Trek — 148
Dhaulagiri Circuit Trek — 156
Dhaulagiri Dolpo Trek — 169
Dhaulagiri Kopra Panorama Trek — 188
Parbat Myagdi Treks — 198
Gurja Himal — 202
Annapurna North Base Camp — 211

APPENDICES — 217
Appendix 1: Trek summaries and suggestions — 217
Appendix 2: Bibliography — 227
Appendix 3: Glossary — 230
Appendix 4: Nepali language hints — 235
Appendix 5: Useful contacts — 237

Maps — 241
About the authors — 248
Other books by the authors — 250

Namaste!

Preface

> It is impossible for any thinking man to look down from a hill on to a crowded plain and not ponder over the relative importance of things.
> ***The Mountain Top*, Frank S Smythe**

Standing aloof and impossibly high, the Himalaya seem to defy reality. Shimmering ice spires and towering ramparts float above fluffy clouds like a painting of the gods. Timeless features of the region are the picturesque villages, multi-coloured hillside terraces and spellbinding valleys. Deep gorges, mysterious forests and wispy woodlands host often-secretive wildlife. Hindu temple bells ring out and the chants of monks sing out from exquisitely located monasteries. Tranquil yak pastures sit below picture-postcard peaks with sweeping snowy faces, fragile, fluted ice walls and glittering glaciers.

All the attractions of Nepal are enchanting, but only on foot can the most appealing inner sanctuaries of the Himalaya be discovered. Mountaineers flock to the highest peaks across the country, including Dhaulagiri. Also on the radar today are Churen Himal, Dhaulagiri II, Tukuche Peak and the peaks of the Hidden Valley, Mukut Himal and Tashigang.

The name Dhaulagiri comes from the local word *dhawala*, meaning dazzling or bright, and *giri* meaning mountain. Dhaulagiri has six different summits.

Apart from the rugged and high altitude Dhaulagiri Circuit trek, very few hikers have explored the greater region surrounding the mountain. Like nearby Annapurna, Dhaulagiri also has a valley that gives access to its inner southern ramparts. The trail is so new that hardly anyone knows about it. Few have trekked into this pristine valley to explore its own hidden sanctuary.

This book is more than a guide to the newest attractions, for they can be described in a few pages. This guide is much more encompassing, endeavouring to give a broader picture of the Dhaulagiri region.

It includes the widest possible choice of treks, all of which give a truer perspective of the mountain Dhaulagiri. Its satellite peaks to the west – Dhaulagiri II, Churen Himal, Putha Hiunchuli and Mukut Himal – stretch as far as Dolpo. To the north is Tukuche Peak and to the east the vast array of summits that form the Annapurna Massif.

With relatively easy access, the new star – the Dhaulagiri Sanctuary Trek – is sure to catch the attention of those seeking a more authentic trekking experience in Nepal. Throughout the greater Dhaulagiri region, countless opportunities exist for long or short treks, for a cultural extravaganza or for a high mountaineering challenge to savour. The communities living in the shadow of Dhaulagiri have long been passed by. Perhaps it's time they too shared in the benefits offered by those trekkers who wish to contribute in a sensitive way to improving the lives of the rural people of the greater Dhaulagiri region.

> How could I say that I wished to penetrate the secrets of the mountains in search of something still unknown that, like the yeti, might well be missed for the very fact of searching?
> ***The Snow Leopard*, Peter Matthiessen**

Siân Pritchard-Jones and Bob Gibbons
Kathmandu 2018

Introduction

The Himalaya of Nepal extend for over 800km from the Indian borders of Sikkim in the east to the Indian Garhwal in the west. They divide the frequently hot, sultry plains of India from the far horizons of the windswept Tibetan plateau. The highest peaks – Kanchenjunga, Makalu, Everest, Lhotse, Manaslu, Annapurna and Dhaulagiri – are located along the northern borders of Nepal. All exceed 8000m in height.

The country of Nepal was isolated for centuries, a forbidden land, seemingly a garden of paradise. Hidden below the Himalaya behind rugged foothills and impenetrable ridges was a lush and plentiful kingdom, locked in a time warp until 1950. The rhythms of life remain intact; the daily rituals, the bonds of religious beliefs and the pace of life roll on with an imperceptible motion. Farmers still plough their small terraced fields while women keep a watchful eye on inquisitive children, intent on new daily discoveries. At higher altitudes the people eke out a hardy living in harsh conditions, where even the vegetation struggles to survive. The people are hardy, hard-working folks, are, endearing, humorous, boisterous, versatile, vibrant and hungry for change, just like most people across the planet. Progress has begun to change the region, as new dirt roads snake along the deep gorges.

The trails are varied and enticing, some criss-cross the intricately sculptured terraces and hillsides, while others head into cool, refreshing forests of bamboo and exotic rhododendron. Just a few of the trails contour gently along, defined by enthusiastic guides as 'Nepali flat', but that is a misnomer since most are never level. In the lower hills you may glimpse a Hindu god worshipped with fervent devotion at a wayside shrine. Climbing higher, wispy lichens and goblinesque woodlands give way to pine and larch, disturbed only by gentle breezes. Higher trails lead to silent alpine glades and rugged, high mountain desert. Up here the mesmerising chants of the monks and the intoxicating roar of a Tibetan horn at dawn may be your early morning call.

Visitors come to Nepal for many, sometimes unfathomable reasons, including these authors!

For most it is the magical Himalaya range; others come for the challenge of climbing the peaks. Some seek a more intimate connection with the country – meeting the colourful people and watching their festivals. The architectural wonders of the Kathmandu Valley, where history and whimsical, fairytale-like images stare the mesmerised guest in the face, provide the opening scene of this magnificent unfolding drama. Discerning travellers come to learn about the mystical religious life of the country, where a myriad of enigmatic sights will baffle and intrigue even the most non-spiritual soul.

Some will venture in search of the fabulous diversity of the flora, while others, with endless patience, seek out the fauna – the fleet-of-foot Himalayan tahr, a red panda or the elusive snow leopard. The birds of the Himalaya are legendary, with beautiful but skittish kingfishers along the riverbanks, colourful danfe pheasants in the mountains and ravenous carrion-eating Himalayan griffons and lammergeyers in the skies. Whatever the reasons for a visit to Nepal, no one should leave disappointed. Trekkers are sure to be smitten by these magical places, leaving with a renewed inspiration for life.

The greater Dhaulagiri area is a trekkers' paradise, where people are always eager to welcome visitors. The mountain drama holds trekkers spellbound. Finely fluted faces and gigantic, jagged ridges defy the imagination. The valleys sing only to the tunes of soaring predatory vultures. Placid blue lakes lie serenely below glaciers that speak to the gods, giving inspiration and renewal to a jaded spirit. On the southern slopes the countryside is lush, fertile and alive with life. Far below towards the Indian border are the endless lapis-coloured blue ridges of the middle hills.

Dhaulagiri Sanctuary Trek

Until a small research party from the Myagdi Chamber of Commerce/Himalayan Map House/NTB/TAAN and VITOF (Tourism Promotion Forum Nepal) trekked deeper into the pristine southern valley of Dhaulagiri in 2016, only local herders knew that a route existed to the heart of the peak. During that reconnaissance the route from Phedi into the Sanctuary was virtually barred by tortuous cliffs and water-drenched canyons.

Following the Raghuganga Khola valley from the Magar village of Jhi, the trail initially crosses timeless farming hillsides high above the snaking valley. Approaching the vast ramparts of Dhaulagiri, the route forges a way around the guarding canyon and towering cliffs on a new trail to gain the icy domain of the Sanctuary. This abode of the gods is utterly dominated by the soaring (4000m) south face of Dhaulagiri. Here is a hidden paradise that is virtually encircled by peaks; Manapati (6380m) and Jirbang (6062m) loom to the west.

Mainly Magar and Chantyal people inhabit the lower foothills of Dhaulagiri. Most are Hindu, although some Buddhists also call this valley home. Quaint traditional farmhouses, terraced fields and a sprinkling of temples dot the landscape. The daily rhythms of life remain almost untroubled by the outside world; the routines interrupted only by many colourful festivals (and now by mobile phones!). This guide includes background detail about the culture of the region, which we hope will enlighten trekkers, bringing added enjoyment and knowledge to their trek.

Dhaulagiri Sanctuary Plus Trek

Until the trail improvements have been completed, this option is only for those with some mountaineering experience, and probably only in November when the pass should be snow-free. This extended version of the Dhaulagiri Sanctuary trek crosses the Ruwachaur Himal ridge south of the peak of Sarbang Dhuri (4991m). Used only by summer herders and foresters, this pass (est 4500m) is reached from Phedi (2466m) in the Raghuganga valley. A very long and ill-defined route (2000m) descends to Lete in the Kali Gandaki valley. The panoramic views of the Nilgiri peaks, Annapurna I, Fang and Annapurna South are sure to be mesmerising. Taking this option makes a circular route sure to tantalise any mountaineering trekker.

The area is devoid of lodges, with only a few homestays on offer until reaching the Kali Gandaki valley. Camping is still the only means with which to get to the actual Sanctuary and across the pass to Lete. Various options for the return route exist from Lete.

The simplest choice is to follow the Kali Gandaki to Tatopani and return to Pokhara via Ghorepani, Birethanti or Ghandruk. Another option is to follow the route from above Galeshwar near Beni up through Nangi to Ghorepani. The never-ending ascending trail from Tatopani via the Barah Danda ridge to the Kopra ridge is a more rugged choice. Others might just take a bus to Pokhara for a 'proper' holiday!

Dhaulagiri Circuit Trek

Until now this was the only trek taken by tough hikers wanting to explore the hidden valleys and the upper snowy plateau of Dhaulagiri. It's still only a route for those with some mountaineering experience, as it crosses high snowbound passes, edging around tumbling glaciers. The route climbs from Darbang along the Myagdi Khola valley to the high altitude canyons on the west side of the peak. Crossing the two 5000m+ passes of French Pass and Dhampus Pass, the route is subject to harsh icy conditions and unpredictable weather. That said, the challenges provided are exciting, inspiring and, yes, a little formidable. This trek is sometimes called Around Dhaulagiri.

Dhaulagiri Dolpo Trek

Only for those with weeks of time, this trek combines the Guerrilla Trek route along the southern flanks of Dhaulagiri and Churen Himal and eastern Dolpo. Accessed from Pokhara via Beni and Darbang, the route crosses ridges and forest. After Dhorpatan the trail crosses the Jang La Pass to Tarakot. From here two options are possible. The easier choice climbs to Dho Tarap in Dolpo and then crosses the exciting passes of the Jharkoi La and Mo La to reach Chharka. The full circuit of the Dhaulagiri Massif returns east via the high and panoramic views of the Jungben La to Kagbeni and Jomsom in the Kali Gandaki valley. Those with experience and a mountaineering support crew can complete the circular route via the little-known Bharbung Khola and Mukut valley. Mountaineering experience is required to cross the Mukut La to join the first option above Chharka. An even more ambitious (and more costly) option from Chharka heads into Upper Mustang (US$500 permit required) via the Ghami La pass.

Dhaulagiri Kopra Panorama Trek
The high and airy ridge of the Kopra Danda is perhaps one of the best vantage points from which to appreciate the drama and inspiring form of Dhaulagiri. Views are sensational across the Kali Gandaki to the mountain, with its stunning companions – Churen Himal, Tukuche Peak and Dhampus Peak. Long a favourite in the 1980s and 90s with camping trekkers, this route is now graced by homestays and lodges. The lower trails are a delight through Ghandruk and Tadapani. Higher up the route crosses quiet slopes below Annapurna South, giving some much desired peaceful forest and upland meadow walking. Ever higher on the southwest shoulder of Annapurna South, the views open. Kopra Ridge is surely one of the most amazing lofty perches in Nepal.

Parbat Myagdi Treks
Offering a completely different sort of experience, these two short and easier options showcase the culture of the region. Within sight of Dhaulagiri for most of the time, these homestay-based treks combine rural village life and quiet forests with panoramic views. New little-used roads will make itineraries shorter, but in essence the treks remain a window on the daily life of the people. One new route being planned is the Karbakeli Trek that explores the home of the Pun Magar people west of Poon Hill.

Gurja Himal Trek
A very secretive area, these newly developed trekking options are located west of Beni and Darbang below the out-lying peak of Gurja Himal, part of the main Dhaulagiri II, Churen Himal and Putha Himal massif. The lower areas are characterised by quaint untouched villages such as Gurjakhani. Mining was once the main occupation here, along with farming. The region is home to the Chantyal people as well as the Magars. Being so isolated, they have developed a unique culture with unusual dances and faith.

Annapurna North Base Camp Trek

Another trek in the greater region close to Dhaulagiri, this route also promises to offer sensational panoramic views. Although the trail is yet to be rebuilt following the years since the 1950 Herzog Annapurna expedition, plans are in place to open this route. Those coming from the Dhaulagiri Sanctuary via the Ruwachaur ridge to Lete or Kalopani might want to take in part of the route. The trail climbs to the Thulobugin ridges before descending to Dana near Tatopani. When the trail to the North Base Camp of Annapurna I finally opens, this route will soon become the 'new place to go' – the envy of those who have, until now, only been able to glance skywards to its inviting bastions.

****

This book also includes detailed sections about the local people encountered and their colourful culture. The Dhaulagiri region offers all styles of trekking, with cosy lodge trips, local homestay opportunities, camping options where only a full crew will make the journey possible, as well as rugged mountaineering options.

Of course any venture into untamed and wild places presents some risks and dangers. A trek to the remote Himalayan regions needs careful preparation and Informed planning by any prospective visitor. Part of this guide is devoted to those aspects.

The main aim of this guidebook is to inspire the readers to go beyond the familiar, to discover the treasures of Nepal – its mountains, its people and its culture. That 'once-in-a-lifetime' trek to Nepal is likely to be life-changing and habit-forming!

> I remember looking over the Himalaya and not feeling that I had closed the door on exploration, but rather just the opposite. I remember thinking, 'God, the possibilities are endless – this range will never be fully explored.' It looks like I was right.
> **Sir Edmund Hillary**

BEFORE THE TREK

Country background

Geography
It is believed that a sea existed about 100 million years ago in the region of Nepal. According to the theory of plate tectonics, India and Tibet began to collide at least 50 million years ago. These plates within the earth's crust create mountains where they collide. Approximately 40–45 million years ago, the northbound Indian plate began to force up the Tibetan plateau. The Himalayan chain was formed some 20 million years ago and continues to rise to this day.

From the Hindu Kush ranges of Afghanistan and Pakistan in the west to the Indian states of Arunachal Pradesh in the east, the Himalaya form an unbroken chain of over 2500km that divides the plains of India from the Tibetan plateau. The country of Nepal is approximately 800km long and 250km in width, with some variations from east to west. Kanchenjunga, Makalu, Everest, Lhotse, Manaslu, Annapurna and Dhaulagiri, all exceeding 8000m in height, are the country's highest peaks.

Rising abruptly from the plains of India are the steep but fragile Siwalik Hills. The forested Mahabharat Hills, towering to over 3000m, mark the southern edge of the middle hills of Nepal, where most of the rural population live. The rolling hills are characterised by impressive terraces and dotted with quaint farmhouses. The valleys of Kathmandu and Pokhara are in this area. Further north are the rocky buttresses and sheer-sided canyons that form the immediate foundations of the great ice peaks. The main Himalayan range is not a watershed but is cut by raging, fast-flowing rivers that allow access to the higher valleys. The watershed is north of the Nepal Himalaya in Tibet.

The altitude range varies from 600m to 8848m, the summit of Everest, although most trekkers will reach a maximum height of 5550m. Trails are rarely undulating or flat, so all visitors need to be relatively fit for a trek here in Nepal.

Climate

> ... and the clouds, they are so beautiful.
> **The Sorcerer of the Clouds, Yan Giezendanner**

The climate of Nepal is influenced heavily by the Himalaya, a natural barrier that divides the main weather systems of Asia. The Indian plains to the south are generally hot and dry, while north India has cooler, high pressure-dominated winters. During the northern summer, the humid monsoon brings life-sustaining rains to India. North of the Himalaya, the mountains create a rain-shadow, making the climate in Tibet sunny, but harsh, cold and windy. As a general rule, throughout autumn and spring, the temperatures on the southern slopes of the Himalaya range from 10°C to 30°C. North of the great mountain barrier, the temperature will range from 15°C down to -10°C and colder at night. The spring season after early April will have generally higher temperatures and more wind. During the monsoon, temperatures rarely dip below freezing, except in the highest meadows. Annual precipitation is normally less than 500 millimetres.

Singing in the rain!

"Regard as one this life, the next life, and the life between," wrote Milarepa. And sometimes I wonder into which life I have wandered – so still are the long nights here, and so cold.
The Snow Leopard, **Peter Matthiessen**

Natural history

Plants

With so many climatic zones, Nepal is a paradise for botanists – no one can be surprised by the great variety of plants, recently estimated to exceed 6500 different types of grasses, plants, flowers, and trees. In the 19th century the noted botanist, Joseph Hooker, visited the Himalaya of Sikkim and eastern Nepal, and discovered many of the plants now familiar to gardeners the world over. The plants found in Nepal are naturally similar to those of neighbouring Sikkim.

> He told them tales of bees and flowers, the ways of trees, and the strange creatures of the Forest, about the evil things and the good things, things friendly and things unfriendly, cruel things and kind things, and secrets hidden under brambles.
> *The Lord of the Rings*, **J R R Tolkien**

Amazing rhododendrons

The lowland slopes and steamy jungles of the Siwalik hills bordering the Indian plains are home to sal trees, simal, sissoo, khair and mahogany. Behind these rapidly eroding sandy foothills are the sheer and abruptly rising Mahabharat ranges. Here are the ubiquitous pipal and banyan trees that shade the frequent porter rest-stops (*chautara*). Chestnut, chilaune and bamboo are found here, while in the succulent cloud forests are an amazing variety of weepy lichens, ferns, rattans and dripping lianas. Prolific orchids, magnolia, broadleaf temperate oak and rhododendron (locally called *Laliguras*) drape the higher hillsides.

Orchids

Further up the hillsides are spruce, chir pine, fir, hemlock, blue pine, larch, cedar and sweet-smelling juniper. Poplar and willow are found along streams in the higher reaches of the arid zones and in the highest pastures are hardy berberis and stunted juniper.

Even higher are caragana, cotton trees, cotoneaster and, fleetingly, honeysuckle. Hardy flowers and plants, such as colourful gentians, survive in even the most windswept or icy meadows. Surprisingly, some shrubs like rhododendron survive better on the north-facing slopes, because of the insulation offered by the snow.

Wispy forest trails

Animals

> The spell of silence on this place is warning that no man belongs here.
> ***The Snow Leopard,*** **Peter Matthiessen**

Nepal is home to an incredibly diverse population of mammals, reptiles and birds. The Terai is home to the endangered Asian one-horned rhino, a tough and rugged beast that hides in the tall grasses of the plains and sal forests. Elephants are rarely wild but are used for forest work and to ferry tourists around the national parks in search of the elusive Bengal Tiger, as well as the sloth bear, from a safe vantage point. Spotted deer and sambar deer scurry about in small herds to avoid their predators.

Crocodiles, alligators, the smaller related gharals and marsh mugger lurk in the murky waters of the marshes and rivers that drain further south into the Ganges River. These jungles, once dense, impenetrable and infested by malarial mosquitoes, still host an amazing number of semi-tropical birds. Beyond the lowlands in the middle hills, almost all the hillsides are either covered by undisturbed, dense, spooky forests or are highly developed and extensively cultivated. Yet a great number of animals call these areas home, especially the ones most easily observed, such as the monkeys and langurs that abound in the forests.

At higher elevations the observant trekker will see marmots, pika (a small mouse-like animal, related to the rabbit), mouse hare, Himalayan golden weasel, ermine, dwarf hamster, Tibetan hare, Himalayan hare, Himalayan tahr (a species of large deer) and more often – blue sheep. Tibetan sheep, wolf, wild dog, brown bear and the famed musk deer (a prized trading item, used in perfume and ayurvedic medicine) are rarely seen. Other animals are the kiang (a wild ass), red fox and Tibetan fox. The endangered red panda inhabits the higher reaches too.

Increasingly fewer wild yaks still roam in isolated, remote valleys; most yaks are now domesticated. They can live for 15–20 years and are mature by 4–5 years. Yak (nak) milk is used by herders to produce cheese and yoghurt (some sun-dried). The dzo – a cross between a yak and a cow – is commonly used as a pack animal, along with ponies and mules. Herders keep sheep and goats as well as yaks.

Even herders virtually never see the snow leopard. Hunting blue sheep in the dawn or twilight hours, they are extremely wary animals. Big budget television crews have waited years to get any pictures of these beautiful creatures. Let us know if you see a yeti!

Trekkers are almost never likely to encounter dangerous animals in Nepal, although domestic guard dogs can be a menace and quarrelsome yaks should be avoided.

Birds of the Nepalese Himalaya
by Rajendra Suwal, ecologist

Nepal is a fabulous paradise for bird watchers and those keen on sighting the elusive fauna. Within the trekking regions are dense undisturbed forests, high ridges, quiet riverine areas and high barren meadows that have remained much as nature intended.

Nepal encompasses the Palaearctic in the furthest reaches of the north and the Indo-Malayan realm in the south. It covers ecological regions including Colinean, Montane, Sub-alpine, Alpine and Nival. Rare forest types include Larix griffthiana growing at the timberline. The unique and varied habitats shelter a fantastic diversity of over 400 species of bird species – from the stunning Satyr Tragopan to the spectacular migration of Demoiselle Crane over the frontiers during the autumn and occasionally in spring. Birds move mostly in flocks, hunting insects at different levels in the forest. During quiet times you might spot up to a dozen different species, depending on the season. There are diurnal, crepuscular, nocturnal, seasonal and altitudinal migrants; birds such as the cuckoo visit during the spring for breeding.

At dawn in the forests, the insects stir into life and the insectivores, including the colourful long-tailed minivet, and fire-capped, green-backed, black-lored and black-throated tits, begin their daily foraging. Nectarine, fruit- and berry-eating birds are active soon after dawn. Berries or flowers are tempting magnets for multiple species, including whiskered, stripe-throated, rufous-naped and white-browed tits.

The dense forests are good places to observe the great parrotbill, spotted laughing thrush, and the velvet, rufous-bellied and white-tailed nuthatch. Try to catch a glimpse of the golden-breasted, white-browed and rufous-winged fulvetta. The forests are full of red-tailed, rufous-tailed and blue-winged minla. The tapping of the rufous-bellied, crimson-breasted and pied woodpeckers invariably interrupts the silence. The forests are alive with the beautiful scarlet, spotted and great rose finch, along with the spot-winged grosbeak. Keen birdwatchers will be amazed to see tiny warblers, including the chestnut-crowned, Whistler's, black-faced, grey-hooded and ashy-throated warblers. Nepal cutia is found in forests of alder.

The flowering trees host smart sunbirds as well as the black-throated, green-tailed, fire-tailed and purple sunbird. Fire-breasted flowerpeckers are found near settlements, in the flowering trees and mistletoe. Large-billed crows scavenge on kitchen leftovers or raid village crops.

Flocks of red and yellow-billed chough forage around farms or high above the passes. The olive-backed pipit, magpie, robin and common tailorbird are found near farms, along with the common stonechat and the grey, collared, white-tailed and pied bushchat.

The idyllic, quiet, often dreamy riverbanks and side streams are teeming with frisky birds. The pristine environments are very rewarding habitat for river birds, including white-capped water redstart and plumbeous redstart; little, spotted, black-backed and slaty-backed forktail; brown dipper, grey wagtail and blue whistling-thrush. Other common birds are the red-vented and black bulbul, great and blue-throated barbet, and also coppersmith barbet in the lower reaches. On the overhanging cliffs are the rarely seen honeycombs made by the world's largest honeybees, where you may spot the oriental honeyguide.

Ravens are acrobatic birds, seen in the alpine zones. The blue pine woodlands of the high ridges are the typical habitat of the very vocal spotted nutcracker, while orange-bellied leafbirds prefer the upper canopies. More treasures are the tiny Nepal, scaly-breasted and pygmy wren babblers, feeding under the ferns, with their high-pitched territorial calls. With its high-pitched sound, the jewel-like, tiny chestnut-headed tesia is a wonderful bird to see in moist undergrowth.

The mountains and forests harbour pheasant species, namely the Danfe, Kalij, Satyr Tragopan and Blood Pheasant. Shy by nature, one can hear them before dawn. In the rhododendron and oak forest, just below the tree line, look out for ringal, and in cane bamboo watch for the satyr tragopan and blood pheasant. The Himalayan munal (known as Danfe in Nepal, where it is the national bird), favours the tree line and more open pastures.

The trans-Himalayan valleys are flyways for migrating birds of prey. Eagles (steppe and imperial) and cinereous vulture, small birds of prey, pied and hen harriers and common buzzards may be seen flying past in the first two weeks of November. Watch for the northern raven and the migratory black-necked cranes.

The skies host the Himalayan and Eurasian griffon and majestic lammergeyer (with 3m wingspans). As they soar, they lift every onlooker's spirit. Cliffs are breeding sites for vultures and lammergeyers. All the vulture species of Nepal, including the Egyptian vulture, the endangered white-rumped, the red-headed and the globally endangered slender-billed vulture, are found in the foothills. A formidable predator of the high mountains is the Golden Eagle. In the caragana bush, look for the white-browed tit-babbler, white-throated, Guldenstadt's and blue-fronted redstart, and brown, rufous-breasted and Altai accentor. Rock bunting and chukor partridge inhabit areas between the upper forested zone and the drier regions. In the air you can observe the speedy insect-hunter white-rumped needletail, Nepal house martin, red-rumped swallow and Himalayan swiftlet.

Finally, in the areas adjacent to the highest ridges look for lively Himalayan snowcocks and flocks of snow pigeons foraging near trails, oblivious of rare passing climbers.

Rajendra Narsingh Suwal
Rajendra holds a Master's Degree in Science (Zoology/Ecology) and has three decades of experience in conservation, ornithological research, wetland conservation and eco-tourism. In 1984 he began his career as a naturalist in Chitwan National Park; it has continued unabated with wildlife studies and research projects. He worked as an ornithological consultant for the National Trust for Nature Conservation (NTNC) and for WWF Nepal. He also worked with the KGH Group of Hotels. With Nepal Nature dot com Travels, he guided ex-president Jimmy Carter on bird-watching trips to Nepal. His expertise has been invaluable to the BBC on various documentaries, including the famed Planet Earth series. Currently he is Deputy Director at WWF Nepal.

See also Bird Conservation Nepal www.birdlifenepal.org

Brief history

Nepal is one of the most diverse places on earth, its culture and people as varied as its scenic attractions. Kathmandu, with its long history of isolation, is the country's once-mystical capital. Its ancestry is an improbable cocktail of magical make-believe, exotic folklore, intriguing legend and historical fact.

The Kiranti people were probably the first recognisable inhabitants of the Kathmandu Valley. However, the first known historical facts in Nepal relate to the formation of the Buddhist religion. Around 550BC, in southern Nepal close to modern-day Lumbini, a prince, who would have an amazing impact across the Indian subcontinent and as far away as Japan, was born to a rich king. This prince, Siddhartha Gautama, who would become the earthly Buddha, lived a sheltered and indolent life in his comfortable palace. Tormented by his lifestyle, he left his wife and newborn son to search for the meaning of life. Seeking out sages, sadhus, priests and wise men, he found no answers until finally his meditations brought a ray of light. He discovered that the end to earthly suffering was achieved through adopting a middle path in all things and thus he found inner peace – nirvana.

Indian Emperor Ashoka, one of the first emissaries of Buddhism in India, travelled to Nepal in the third century BC, building the four ancient grass-covered stupas of Patan and the pillar at Lumbini. After about 300AD the Licchavi dynasty flourished, but Buddhism declined in the face of the popular rise of the Hindu religion, a faith that had been born, but not nurtured, much earlier in India. Much later, as new trade routes and ideas developed between Tibet and India, Kathmandu became the most important Himalayan hub.

On the religious front, the decline of Buddhism in India and Nepal forced its diehard adepts to seek sanctuary across the Himalaya in Tibet. After hundreds of years, the version of Buddhism that came with those refugees adapted and absorbed Tibetan Buddhist themes and, ironically, slipped back once more into Nepal to mix with Hinduism, Shamanism and other animistic beliefs. The Tibetan version of Buddhism, now known as the Vajrayana path, provides an astonishingly colourful and exotic aspect to daily rituals and festivities in Nepal today.

In the 8th century a sage and Buddhist master, Padma Sambhava (Guru Rinpoche), travelled across the Himalayan region. His exploits in propagating the Tibetan Buddhist philosophy are recorded widely throughout the region as both myth and historical fact.

During the following period there are few records of life in Nepal. However, through the annals kept in Tibet, a great amount of historical fact can be found about the regeneration of the Buddhism found in Nepal. These facts centre on the ancient Tibetan region of the lost Guge Kingdom, located around Toling and Tsaparang. Many Indian masters came here to study and escape persecution from Hindu zealots in the 11th century.

Records of Nepal's history come to life again in the 13th century, when the Malla kings assumed power. The Malla Period is often said to be the golden age of Nepal, and especially of the Kathmandu Valley, with its astonishing array of art and architecture. The Malla dynasties are admired for their vast concentration of elaborate and superbly executed multi-tiered palaces and pagodas. Although the ordinary people lived in much less privileged conditions, their brick houses were also decorated with intricate wood designs. One of the more powerful Mallas, Jayasthiti Malla, adopted the Hindu faith and consolidated his power in the Kathmandu Valley. He even declared himself to be a reincarnate of the Hindu god of preservation, Vishnu, a practice that was continued by the monarchs of Nepal until 2007. Jyoti Malla and Yaksha Malla were rather more benign dictators, who enhanced the valley with more spectacular temples and religious structures.

Around 1482 the three towns of Kathmandu, Patan and Bhaktapur became independent cities, with each king competing to build the greatest Durbar Square, parts of which remain to this day.

Like all dictatorships, the Malla reign declined, as debauchery and corruption took hold. In 1769, from the hilltop fortress above the town of Gorkha (Gurkha), came Prithvi Narayan

Shah and his forces, who rode in to capture the three cities of the Kathmandu Valley. In so doing he succeeded in unifying Nepal. In 1788 Nepalese armies moved on Tibet, but a vast army from China intervened to help the Tibetans repulse them.

In 1816 the Gurkhas, attempting to expand their domains into the colonial-ruled hills of northern India, were defeated by the British. Through the treaty of Segauli, Nepal ceded Sikkim to India and the current borders were delineated. The British established a resident office in Kathmandu. Soon after, Gurkha regiments were integrated into the British army.

In 1846, Jung Bahadur Kunwar Rana, a soldier of the court, hatched a devious plot. After a massacre in Kathmandu's Kot Square, the king was dethroned and the queen was sent into exile. Jung Bahadur Rana took power and became the first of the infamous Rana dynasty, who held power in Nepal for the next 100 years. They were despotic rulers, remembered for family intrigues, murder and deviousness. Calling themselves Maharajas, they built the sumptuous neo-colonial white colonnaded palaces seen around Kathmandu today. Until 1950 the country remained closed to all but a few invited guests, retaining its mediaeval traditions and corrupt governance. When neighbouring India gained independence in 1947, a Congress Party was formed in Kathmandu. The powerless king became a symbol for freedom from the despotic Ranas. However, freeing the country from the shackles of the old guard meant great sacrifice. Many activists and freedom fighters were executed before King Tribhuvan finally ousted the Ranas in 1951.

After 1950, when Tibet fell under new masters, refugees and Khampa freedom fighters moved into the isolated valleys in the north of the Himalaya and established bases. Some refugees settled in the region of Rasuwa adjacent to the border. However, when Nepalese monarch King Birendra announced the 'Zone of Peace' initiative, most of the Khampas melted away.

A fledgling democratic coalition government was installed and the country was opened to foreign visitors. In May 1953 Mount Everest was finally conquered from the Nepalese side after so many failed expeditions from its northern faces in Tibet. King Tribhuvan died in 1955 and his son Mahendra assumed power. Becoming dissatisfied with political paralysis, King Mahendra ended the short experiment with democracy in 1960. He introduced a partyless governance, called the *panchayat* system, based on local councils of five (*panch*) elders, with a tiered system of representatives up to the central parliament. Following the death of Mahendra in 1972, King Birendra inherited the throne. His official coronation had to wait until an auspicious date in the spring of 1975.

The *panchayat* system was retained following the 1980 referendum. After 1985, rapid urban expansion changed the nature of the Kathmandu Valley. The traditional rural lifestyle began to disappear under a wave of construction as the population grew astronomically. In April 1990 full-scale rioting and demonstrations broke out, forcing the king to allow full democracy. Parliamentary democracy flourished with King Birendra as a ceremonial monarch and the country prospered. Unfortunately corruption and political ineptitude grew, and in the late nineties a grass-roots Maoist rebellion developed.

Many people had genuine sympathy with the need for greater social equality, but violent demands for a leftist dictatorship naturally met with resistance. In June 2001, after a tragic shooting spree, King Birendra and almost his entire family were wiped out by his son, Crown Prince Dipendra. Although not directly attributed to the Maoist uprising, the event changed the situation dramatically. King Birendra's brother Gyanendra became king, but in October 2002 he dissolved parliament and appointed his own government until elections could be held. The Maoist rebellion continued, with intimidation and coercion rife in the countryside. Following huge demonstrations on the streets of Kathmandu in 2006, King Gyanendra relinquished power.

The Maoist leaders entered mainstream politics after winning a majority in the subsequent election. However, almost ever since then, the governments have been paralysed, with a political stalemate derailing much development. A constitutional election was held in November 2013 with the Maoist vote significantly reduced. A new constitution was promulgated in September 2015 but it remains to be seen where the country's ruling elite will take it.

Political and economic instability have resulted in an increasing number of young Nepalese seeking work outside the country, particularly in the Arabian Gulf and Malaysia. Tourism also remains an important source of income and tourists are still given a warm welcome across the country.

Religion and festivals

> Holy places never had any beginning. They have been holy from the time they were discovered...
> **The Land of Snows, Giuseppe Tucci**

Life across Nepal is still significantly influenced by religious and traditional beliefs. Everywhere, from a hilltop monastery to the back-alleys of Kathmandu, people follow cultural traditions through daily rituals and frequent festivals.

Hinduism

Hinduism is the main faith of Nepal and until recently the country was a Hindu kingdom. Many Hindu ideals have come from the ancient Indian Sanskrit texts, the four Vedas. In essence, the ideas of Hinduism are based on the notion that everything in the universe is connected. This means that one's deeds in this life will have a bearing on the next. One's own bad actions might be the cause of misfortune. Natural disasters are seen as the vengeance of the gods. Although hundreds of Hindu gods exist, they are in essence one, being worshipped in many different aspects.

The three main Hindu gods are Brahma, the god of creation; Shiva, the god of destruction; and Vishnu, the god of preservation. They appear in many forms, both male and female. Brahma is rarely visible. Shiva has special powers of regeneration and many forms, such as Mahadev, or the dancing Nataraj. Shiva is Pashupati – the Lord of Beasts – and Bhairab in his most destructive form. Shiva's wife is Parvati; she also has many aspects, including Kali and Durga.

The third god, Vishnu, worshipped in Nepal as Narayan, is the preserver of all life. Vishnu has ten avatars. The seventh avatar is Rama, a deity linked to Sita and the Ramayana texts. The eighth is the popular blue god Krishna, who plays a flute and chases after the cowgirls, while the ninth is Buddha.

Other Hindu deities include Lakshmi, the goddess of wealth, and Hanuman, the monkey god.

Sleeping Vishnu on a bed of snakes, Budhanilkanta

Machhendranath is the curious rain deity, the compassionate one with two forms, white (Seto) and red (Rato). Humorous Ganesh, popular with Buddhists as well as Hindus, is worshipped for good fortune.

The trekkers' legend of Ganesh
Ganesh, the elephant-headed god, is the son of Shiva and Parvati. Hindu legends recount that Ganesh was born when Shiva was away trekking. When Shiva returned he saw the child and assumed that Parvati had been unfaithful. In a furious rage, he chopped off Ganesh's head and threw it away. Once Shiva had taken a bucket shower and fortified himself with a cup of rakshi, Parvati explained the matter. In great remorse, Shiva vowed to give Ganesh a new head from the first living being passing; it was an elephant.

Ganesh – a whimsical version from South India looking very healthy and wealthy!

Hindu festivals

Nepal has an extraordinary number of festivals. Any excuse is valid for a good celebration. In autumn, the Dasain and Tihar festivals are in full flow. The goddess Kali and Durga are feted during Dasain, and the terrifying white Bhairab is displayed in Kathmandu Durbar Square. Blood sacrifices are the most noticeable aspect of these celebrations. Tihar is a more light-hearted affair, with crows, dogs, cows and brothers showered with flowers and devotion before a night of fairy lights and candles.

During spring is Shiva Ratri, the night of Shiva, most fervently commemorated at the Pashupatinath temple in Kathmandu. Holi is another Hindu spring festival celebrated across the country. The main manifestation of this festival is the throwing of coloured dyes at passers-by; tourists and trekkers are not excluded! Normally in March the tall wooden chariot housing the white Seto Machhendranath idol – the rain god – is dragged with much merriment through old Kathmandu. Sometimes the power lines are pulled down, adding to the electricity supply problems, and the top storeys of the old brick houses of Asan are almost obliterated. In May, during a similar festival, the red Rato Machhendranath is hauled around Patan and back out to Bungamati.

Buddhism

Buddhists are found in the Kathmandu Valley and in the northern regions of the country. Monasteries are encountered across the mountains. The Buddhist artistry and iconography is startling and is similar to that found in monasteries throughout the high Himalaya.

Buddhism could be considered as a philosophy for living, with adherents seeking to find peace of mind and a cessation of worldly suffering. Nirvana, perfect peace, is achieved through successive lives by good actions and thoughts. (For details of the Sakyamuni, earthly Buddha, see Brief history.) The earthly Buddha is also considered by Hindus to be an incarnation of their god Vishnu.

Buddhism has two main branches; Hinayana and Mahayana. The latter path is followed in Nepal and Tibet, where it has evolved into a more esoteric philosophy called the Vajrayana (Diamond) path. It blends ancient Tibetan Bon ideas with a phenomenon known as Tantra, meaning 'to open the mind'. Tantric themes suggest that all people can become a Buddha and find enlightenment from within.

Tantric Buddhism has many themes, but most involve meditation. Guru Rinpoche was one of Buddhism's greatest Tantric masters. Tantric Yoga is now widely known as one method of pursuing enlightenment. Recently interest has been aroused in ancient exercises, which involve sensual methods of reaching this goal. Curiously, it was the rejection of these liberal themes of Tantric Buddhism that led to the resurgence of Hinduism and the decline of Buddhism in India.

The numerous Buddhist images are not gods, but icons that can be used to direct the mind in meditations towards a true path of learning. The fearsome protectors are not true demons, but remind the follower of their darker side. Other deities can be invoked through meditation to channel the mind's energies towards the search for its true nature. Buddhism has a vast collection of texts and teachings in many forms and aspects.

The following Buddhist sects are found across the country:

The **Nyingma-pa** is the oldest Red Hat sect; it was founded in the eighth century AD by Guru Rinpoche. Today adherents of the Nyingma-pa sect are found across the high Himalaya of Nepal, Tibet, Spiti and Ladakh.

The **Kadam-pa** school was developed by Atisha, a Buddhist scholar from northern India, following his studies at Toling gompa in the Guge region of Western Tibet. Followers are expected to find enlightenment after careful reflection and study of the texts.

The **Kagyu-pa** is attributed to the Indian mystic translator Marpa (1012–1097), a disciple of Atisha. Followers need to concentrate their meditations on spiritual matters and inner mental themes, and listen to the wisdom of their teachers. The Kagyu-pa sect split into a number of sub-groups, such as the Druk-pa, Taglung-pa, Karma-pa and Drigung-pa (see also under Mount Kailash Trek).

The **Sakya-pa** began under Konchok Gyalpo from the Sakya Gompa in Tibet in the 11th century. Its adherents study existing Buddhist scriptures. The Sakya-pa school initiated the creation of the Tangyur and Kangyur – the two great Tibetan Buddhist bibles.

The **Gelug-pa** is the Yellow Hat sect of the Dalai Lama, initiated by the 14th-century reformer, Tsong Khapa. He returned the Buddhist practices to a more purist format, removing the liberal themes of Tantra and putting more emphasis on morality and discipline. The Dalai Lama is regarded by most Buddhists as their spiritual leader.

Guru Rinpoche

Guru Rinpoche (Padma Sambhava) is the most famous icon of Tibetan Buddhism. He was an Indian Tantric master who went to Tibet in the 8th century to help spread the message of the religion there. He established the Nyingma-pa, the oldest sect of the red hats. One of his consorts, Yeshe Tsogyal, wrote down his teachings in order that they could be revealed to future generations. According to legends, Guru Rinpoche visited many places across the Himalaya, meditating in cave retreats and teaching the faith.

Guru Rinpoche, Kobang monastery

Buddhist icon in Yab-Yum, embracing his consort

Buddhist festivals

Losar, the Tibetan New Year, occurs just before the spring in the cold season of January/February. It is primarily celebrated at Boudhanath and also across the northern mountains. Celebrations involve Tibetan drama and colourful masked Cham dances that commemorate the victory of Buddhism over Bon. Many Buddhist festivals related to Tibetan traditions take place in the mountains during the summer monsoon. Buddhists also celebrate Buddha's birthday and the birthday of Guru Rinpoche.

Other Tibetan festivals celebrated across the northern Himalaya are: **Saka Lhuka** held in the first month of the Tibetan calendar; performed for an auspicious harvest; and **Fagnyi**, a week-long festival of song and dance during the seventh Tibetan month.

Festivals of the Dhaulagiri region

The two main festivals of the Magar and Chantyal region are Maghe Sankranti and Shraune Sankranti. The main festival of the region is Purkheuli Naach, which is an ancestral dance strongly defined by the nature worship/animist faith of the area. The Hindu festivals of Dashain, Tihar, Janai Purnima (in August) and Naag Panchami are also celebrated. Some of the dances performed by the people are Ghatu, Kaura, Jhabre, Nacharl, Saleju and Dohori. Most festivities are enjoyed with liberal amounts of Rakshi and Chang. The few Buddhists in the region mark the main occasions like Buddha's birthday, Guru Rinpoche's birthday and Losar, the Tibetan New Year.

Bon or Bonpo

The Bon religion was the earlier faith of Tibet; they also seek the eternal truth and reality of life. The Bon worship natural phenomena like the heavens and mountain spirits, as well as the spirits of natural powers, such as thunder. Many facets and features of Tibetan Buddhism originated from the Bon. The only Bon monastery (and Sowa Rigpa Medical Centre) in the general region is at Chhentung near Dhorpatan, where Tibetan refugees have lived for over 50 years.

There is evidence to suggest that the Bon came not from Tibet but from Olmolungring, a legendary place in Tazik, possibly once in the land of the Tajik people of Central Asia. Tazik is a name that appears in Bon literature. Southwest of Kailash lie the ruins of Khyunglung Ngulkhar – the silver castle of the Khyung bird. This place is believed to be the spiritual and ancestral home of the Bon and the centre of the realm of Shangshung. Not far away are Tirthapuri and the Gurugyam cave monastery, clinging to the side of a sheer cliff, thought to have originally belonged to the Bon.

The first known Bon monastery was founded in 1072 at Yeru Wensakha, which is situated close to the Tsangpo River, just east of Shigatse. It has since fallen into ruin, but other Bon monasteries exist today at Menri, Yungdrung Ling and Tradang. Closer to Nepal, near Mount Shishapangma, is Lake Pekhu Tso, where the Pelha Puk Bon monastery is located on the isolated east side of the lake. A Bon monastery is also located in the Tibetan Kyirong valley between Langtang and Ganesh Himal some 100km north of Kathmandu. As well as Kailash, another major pilgrimage peak is Mount Bonri in southeastern Tibet, close to Mount Namche Barwa, where the Tsangpo River cuts through deep gorges before dropping into India as the Brahmaputra. Most Bon monasteries in Nepal are in Dolpo. In Kathmandu there is one near Swayambhunath – Triten Norbutse. Anyone interested should visit this monastic complex in Kathmandu, such is the rarity of any active Bon culture today.

The ancient Bon believed that all life started from an egg. Within Bon there are many animal-headed demons and deities – many are its protectors. In the Bon masked Cham dances, masks depicting the heads of animals and the protector Khyung-bird are used. The Khyung bird is very reminiscent of the Hindu god, Garuda. The Bon's sacred symbol, the Yungdrung, is very similar to the Tantric Buddhists' dorje, the thunderbolt sceptre. The white yak is particularly revered. The Bon also use the swastika symbol, but theirs turns to the left. The use of prayer flags, the concept of the oracles (trance doctors), and many of their icons have been assimilated into Buddhism. In 1977 the Tibetan government-in-exile in Dharamsala recognised and accepted the Bon as a fifth Tibetan sect. The spiritual head of the Bon is known as Trizin.

The chief icon of the Bon is Tonpa Shenrap Miwoche, who according to legends descended from heaven to earth by way of Mount Kailash. Within the Bon religion there are the 'Four Transcendent Lords': Tonpa Shenrap Miwoche, Shenlha Wokar, Satrig Ersang and Sangpo Bumtri. The deities, both peaceful and wrathful, are used as focal points for adherents to meditate on different aspects in order to understand the whole and reach enlightenment. This idea is used extensively in Buddhism too.

Other prominent deities of Bon include Kuntu Zangpo, who is similar to the Samantabhadra form of the primordial Adi Buddha of Buddhism. He is also a manifestation of Shenlha Wokar, being the 'enlightened one' who is unfettered by possessions. He is depicted in black, together with his white female consort. Kunzang Gyalwa Dupa (Gyatso) is a curious figure, being similar and perhaps a precursor to the thousand-armed Avalokiteshvara, the Tibetan Chenresig deity, of whom the Dalai Lamas are considered incarnates. With nine heads, Welse Ngampa is a wrathful protector representing 'piercing ferocity'. He crushes the enemies of Bon.

Shamanism

With its roots in the mists of time, Shamanism is a difficult religious theme to observe. Much is only apparent through sightings of strange tokens such as bones, feathers and fetish-styled trinkets. Shamans have their own rituals and even medical treatments. These are often performed by *jhankris*/oracles, who communicate with the ancestors through trance-induced rituals. (In the west, *jhankris* are often called *dhami*). Shamans worship natural phenomena, much like the early Bon. Such practices seem very primitive to outsiders, but rely on ancient wisdom. Across Nepal, remnants of ancient forms of animism and shamanism seem to have some influence on both Hindu and Buddhist themes.

Shaman traditions mixed with a brushing of the pre-Buddhist Bon culture are alive and observable in parts of Nepal. Many of their cultural traditions utilise these ancient practices.

Shamans are believed to be able to channel the powers of the earthly gods, but not those of the heavens. In remote parts of the country, some of the shaman gods have been integrated into the local Buddhist faith. In communities where the absence of health posts, legal representation and education is the norm, shamans exercise considerable power. Through animistic means, shamans care for the health and well-being of the community, settle legal disputes and attempt to mitigate the effects of natural disasters.

Other religions in Nepal are Islam, Christianity and Sikhism.

Cultural aspects

Ethnic diversity

According to the latest estimate, the population of Nepal is around 33 million. (In 1974 there were just 8 million.) At least 26 major ethnic groups are encountered across the whole country. Most of the people in the southern zones can be broadly classified as Hindu, while those from the northern Himalayan valleys are Buddhist. However, there is no clear traditional divide in either the middle hills or the Kathmandu Valley, especially since the insurgency.

The **Newari** are the traditional inhabitants of the Kathmandu Valley; they are a mix of Hindu and Buddhist. Along the plains of the Terai are the **Tharu**, whose ancestry might be linked to Rajasthan in India. Other Terai people, also related to Indian Hindu clans, are collectively known as the Madhesi.

Throughout the central regions of Nepal, the people are mainly **Magar, Chhetri, Gurung** and **Brahmin**. The Brahmins are the higher caste priestly group, who traditionally paint their houses blue. Chhetris are defined as a warrior caste. Gurungs are mostly found to the west, around Gorkha, along the Marsyangdi valley and towards Pokhara. Gurung men are particularly noted for their service to the Gurkhas. There is a large concentration of Magars and the smaller sub-clan of the Chantyal in the Myagdi district.

As you climb beyond the central middle hills, the people belong to the **Tibeto-Burmese** ethnic groups, with wide faces and Tibetan characteristics like the **Sherpas**.

The **Tamang** people are almost pure Tibetan stock. They are located right across Nepal, mainly in the northern areas. They live in the country from Taplejung in the east through central, Rasuwa, Nuwakot, Dhading and Lamjung to the far west districts of Humla. Tamangs migrated from Tibet, perhaps as part of the unifying King Srongtsen Gampo's horsemen.

Basic customs

Despite contact with the outside world since 1950, Nepal remains a conservative country, especially in the remoter hilly districts. A few basic customs should be observed by visitors. In houses the cooking area, the hearth and fire should be treated with respect, so do not throw litter there. Never touch a Nepali on the head. Pointing the soles of your feet at your hosts, or stepping over their feet, should be avoided. Eat with your right hand if no utensils are supplied.

Non-believers are rarely allowed into the inner sanctuaries of Hindu temples anywhere in the country; remember that leather apparel, belts and shoes are certainly not permitted inside.

When visiting Buddhist gompas, guests should remove trekking hats and boots before entry. Small donations are appreciated and trekkers should ask permission before taking photographs inside. On the trail, keep to the left of mani walls and chortens and circle them in a clockwise direction. The prolific array of mani walls, mani stones and prayer wheels display the mantra Om Mani Padme Hum – Hail to the Jewel in the Lotus. Bon mani walls and chortens should be circled anti-clockwise.

Begging

The rest of the world often views Nepal as a permanent begging-bowl case. Perhaps it is this attitude that encourages the general malaise of development in the country. Foreign governments, the UN and large donors continue to provide funds, but fail to account for such funding and ignore problems within the system. Inevitably Nepalese view all foreigners as rich, whether it's their governments or themselves. Ordinarily no one will mind giving to those obviously in need, but over the long term local people need to be helped to help themselves.

Begging is not confined to the poverty-stricken lower classes; the other echelons often have the same attitude. Endemic in Nepal, begging is clearly putting a brake on development and local initiative. However, the 'make do and mend' culture shows a level of ingenuity that has almost disappeared in the throwaway societies of the developed world. Given the opportunity, Nepal will flourish and prosper.

Helping the people

The big donor organisations and charities are naturally attracted to Nepal, probably due to its welcoming people, many of whom are exceedingly industrious. Sadly the impact of these multi-national donations is rarely felt by the majority of the people. This means there is plenty of opportunity for guests to contribute to smaller initiatives. Often such projects like improving village water supplies or bringing local electrification can really make a difference. Some of these localised projects are listed below.

Asha Nepal is a human rights organisation working towards the social and economic empowerment of women and children affected by sex trafficking. 'Asha' is the Nepali for 'hope'. (www.asha-nepal.org)

Autism Care Nepal There was very little knowledge of this condition in Nepal when their son was diagnosed with autism, so two Nepali doctors founded this organisation to raise awareness and help others in the same situation.
(www.autismnepal.org)

Beni Handicrafts G*iving Kathmandu's rubbish a new life*
Beni's products are made by women forced to move from the hills to the city, providing them with training, employment and income for their families. They collect sweet wrappers, inner tubes and other waste from the streets of Kathmandu as well as mountain trails. The rubbish is then made into attractive and functional products. View and buy them at the Hotel Moonlight and the Kathmandu Guest House. Profits support the work of **Steps Foundation**. (www.benihandicrafts.com)

Steps Foundation Nepal – Education, Hygiene and Health is a charity supported by profits from Beni Handicrafts. It works on the step-by-step principle that through education for all and increasing awareness of hygiene, the health and well-being of families will be improved. (www.stepsnepal.org)

Community Action Nepal co-founded by mountaineer Doug Scott, seeks to improve the infrastructure of villages in the hills by building schools, health posts, clean water projects and developing cottage industries. (www.canepal.org.uk)

Interburns is an international volunteer network of expert health professionals working to transform global burn care and prevention. Their philosophy is that all burns patients can be provided with good quality care despite limited resources. (www.interburns.org)

International Porter Protection Group (IPPG) began in 1997 after a number of porters suffered unfortunate accidents. It seeks to raise awareness of the conditions and plight of frequently exploited porters. They focus on the shelter, medical care and provision of clothing for often-overlooked porters across Nepal. (www.ippg.net) and (www.portersprogress.org)

Kathmandu Environmental Education Project (KEEP) was established in 1992 to 'provide education on safe and ecologically sustainable trekking methods to preserve Nepal's fragile eco-systems'. They give important information to trekkers, help harness tourism for development, run environmental discussions and manage a porters' clothing bank. They also help to improve the skills of tourism professionals and run volunteer programmes as well as running wilderness first aid training. (www.keepnepal.org)

Mountain People has the motto of 'Helping mountain people to help themselves'. It is a small, independent, non-profit, non-political, non-religious and cross-cultural organisation with a lot of energy and drive. They help with schools, porter welfare, women's projects and bridge building.
(www.mountain-people.org)

So The Child May Live A Liverpool-based charity working to improve paediatric care in Nepal, principally by supporting Kanti Children's Hospital in Kathmandu, the only dedicated children's hospital in Nepal. (www.sothechildmaylive.com)

Destruction or development

There is no doubt that the fragile environment of the Himalaya needs the attention of local environmentalists and the good management of resources. However, much as we, as visitors, may wish to see the land untainted, we do not have to spend our lives shivering beside a smoky fire. Inevitably, if there is no viable reason for the youth to linger in the high Himalayan regions, the culture will be diluted.

Tourism is one obvious way in which the culture and livelihoods of the upland people can be sustained in the long term. The main trekking trails have already had almost sixty years of tourism and the effects have been generally positive. The difficulty is finding the right balance, by improving local living conditions without destroying that which every visitor wants to experience here.

It's not a unique problem, as anyone who has visited the popular Nepalese trails or anywhere else that attracts many visitors – even Chamonix or Machu Picchu – will have observed. Ultimately it is for the local people and the various tourism concerns to decide on the future of their region.

Rural development through tourism

Practicalities

Time and calendar

> … eternity is not remote, it is here beside us.
> ***The Snow Leopard,* Peter Matthiessen**

Nepal is 5hrs 45mins ahead of GMT. Nepal follows two calendars; the Gregorian calendar used by most of the world, and a lunar-solar Bikram Sambat (BS) calendar, which is approximately 56 years and 8 months ahead of the Gregorian dates. (i.e. 2018–19 corresponds to 2074–76 BS). The Bikram Sambat year begins in mid-April and was introduced by the Ranas in the mid-1800s. This calendar means that Nepal is ahead of the rest of the world, which it might be in terms of coping with adversity!

Getting to Nepal

Flights to Nepal

The following airlines serve Nepal from Europe, Southeast Asia, the Pacific, Australia and North America.

Air Arabia and **Fly Dubai** from The Gulf; **Air Asia** budget flights from Kuala Lumpur; **Air India** via Delhi, Kolkata (Calcutta) and Varanasi; **Bangladesh Biman** via Dhaka; **Chinese airlines** from Lhasa, Xianyang, Chengdu, Kunming and Guangzhou (Canton); **Dragon Air** from Hong Kong; **Druk Air/Royal Bhutan Airlines** from Paro, Bhutan, to Kathmandu and on to Delhi; **Etihad Airways** via Abu Dhabi from Europe; **Jet Airways** (India) has a through-service from London to Nepal via Delhi and Bombay; **Korean Airlines** from the Far East; **Nepal Airlines** flies from Delhi, Bombay, Dubai and Hong Kong – for those with bags of time; **Oman Airways** via Muscat; **Silk Air** from Singapore; **SpiceJet** and **Indigo** low-cost Indian carriers; **Himalayan Airlines** has services to the Gulf; **Thai Airways** via Bangkok, from Europe and Australia/New Zealand; **Qatar Airways** via Doha from Europe; **Turkish Airlines** via Istanbul from Europe; plus **Virgin, BA** and other airlines to Delhi, then one of the Indian carriers to Kathmandu. This information is subject to change.

Overland routes to Nepal

Nepal has open land borders with India and Tibet/China. Land borders into Nepal from India are through Sonauli/Belahiya near Bhairahawa; Raxaul/Birgunj; Nepalganj; Mahendranagar; and Kakarvitta. The Sonauli/Belahiya border north of Gorakhpur is the most-used entry point from India. Buses connect Bhairahawa to Kathmandu and Pokhara. A long journey by local transport links Nepal to Delhi in the west, through Mahendranagar/Banbasa. Those travelling between Kathmandu and Darjeeling or Sikkim can cross the eastern border at Kakarvitta.

Kathmandu is also linked to Lhasa in Tibet by the new highway through the border at Rasuwa/Kyirong. The road is generally tarred to Lhasa but poor on the Nepalese side near Dhunche in the Langtang area. The 5–6 day journey to Lhasa will blow your mind. It climbs over a number of spectacular 5000m passes through Lhatse, Shigatse and Gyangtse to Tibet's once-forbidden capital, Lhasa. Unfortunately the original route via Barhabise, Zhangmu and Nyalam was badly affected by the 2015 earthquake and has not yet reopened; it remains to be seen if overland travel will restart on this route.

Travel within Nepal

Travel within Nepal is possible either by road or by air.

Bus and jeep

Road transport can be on a noisy, crowded public bus, a so-called 'tourist bus', or in a privately hired jeep or car. It's a compromise between comfort, safety, time taken and money spent.

Travelling between Kathmandu and Pokhara (200km) by bus is quite straightforward these days, since the road has been improved almost all the way. The usual journey time is 6–8hrs, but traffic can get heavy in the afternoon if you are heading back to Kathmandu. Currently the most luxurious bus is the Greenline service: US$25 including a good lunch halfway at the Riverside Springs Resort. Other slightly less deluxe (but generally reliable) tourist buses depart around 7am from various points. The Swiss Travels bus is a long-standing option.

More unreliable, and definitely not comfortable, are the 'local' buses, which are even cheaper and leave from the Gongabu bus depot, northwest of the city. These are only recommended for those wishing to rub shoulders intimately with the locals. Ironically the taxi fare to the bus station is normally more than the bus ticket, so there is little to recommend this option. The local buses often stop in Mugling, an infamous eating place which, in days gone by, served dishes of 'hepatitis and rice'.

Road travel to places further afield can be long and tiring. Routes go via the Terai lowlands to the trekking areas of Kanchenjunga and Makalu to the east, and West Nepal and Dolpo to the west. Jeep dirt roads are pushing into previously remote areas with amazing speed. Don't expect a comfortable ride on often-dreadful tracks.

Internal flights

Operated by a few local airlines, the main routes are to Pokhara, Nepalganj and Biratnagar. The main mountain routes are to Lukla (for Everest) and Jomsom (for Mustang and the Annapurna Circuit). Other sectors with less frequent services are to Tumlingtar (for Makalu and the Arun Valley route to Everest) and Taplejung/Suketar (for Kanchenjunga).

Further away flights head to Juphal/Dunai (for Dolpo) and Simikot (for Rara Lake, Saipal and the Limi Valley). Flights are subject to delays caused by weather and occasionally by other 'Nepalese' factors. The price for foreigners is higher than for locals. Helicopters are becoming quite common for sightseeing charters as well as rescue missions. Prices range from OK to sky high!

Visa information

Nepalese visa

www.nepalimmigration.gov.np

All foreign nationals except Indians require a visa. Currently visas are available from embassies and land borders, as well as at Tribhuvan International Airport on arrival in Kathmandu (check for any changes before arrival). Entering or exiting the country at the remoter crossing points and from Tibet may be subject to change, so always check the latest requirements in all cases. Applying in your own country will cost more. Remember to apply well ahead of travel, in case there are any holidays at the embassy due to festival periods in Nepal.

Obtaining a visa on arrival is normally the easiest option, but check in case of any new restrictions. To save time at the airport, fill in the preliminary form online at home and print off the bar code. The maximum length of stay in Nepal is five months in one calendar year; the fifth month is not always possible. Tourist visas are available for 15, 30 or 90 days, at a fee of $25, $40 and $100 (payment in cash) respectively.

Extensions in Kathmandu are obtained at the Immigration Department at a cost of $US30 (the minimum fee, for 15 days) or for a daily charge of $US2 per day. Recently the rules have changed, and anyone requiring a visa extension in Kathmandu must go online and fill in the forms in advance, uploading a passport-style photo. Using the machine in the immigration hall is free of charge, but likely to be time-consuming and rather hard to fathom.

All visas are currently multiple-entry, making visits to places like Bhutan, Tibet or India much easier than before. Check the up-to-date fees at www.nepalimmigration.gov.np. For comprehensive embassy listings, see: www.mofa.gov.np

Indian visa

Allow at least 7–10 days if you intend to get your Indian visa in Kathmandu and expect delays. It is currently much cheaper to do this in your home country than in Nepal. Fees in Kathmandu vary from US$50–$190 depending on nationality. E-visas are now available online; cheaper and easier! Do check the visa situation before travel; change is likely at any time! www.indianembassy.org.np

Tibet/China entry

For those planning a trip to Tibet/China from Nepal after a trek, it's currently of no use to obtain a Chinese visa in advance. The Chinese visa will simply be cancelled at the Kathmandu embassy, because travel to Tibet from Nepal currently requires special arrangements. It is necessary to prearrange the visa for Tibet in Nepal through a Nepalese agent. Allow a few days in Kathmandu to complete application well ahead of your arrival in Nepal if prearranging by email. Visas for travel across Tibet are normally issued on paper for the duration of the stated itinerary. Budget (not that cheap) tours are offered by Kathmandu travel agents for independent travellers, thus making that fabulous trip a possibility. The Chinese authorities frequently close the Tibetan border at short notice. Following the earthquakes of spring 2015, the border road to Tibet via Zhangmu was closed. A new border post at Rasuwa near Syabrubesi, Langtang area, has been built and opened for tourists. Do check for the latest information before planning a trip.

Money matters

> I now add worry about the cash supply to my collection of other possible misfortunes.
> ***Stones of Silence*, George Schaller**

The currency is the Nepalese Rupee (Rs). Notes come in the following denominations: Rs5, 10, 20, 50, 100, 500 and 1000, and occasionally coins: Rs1, 2 and 5.

Approximate exchange rates (Feb 2019)	
	Rs
£	142
€	122
US$	109
CHF	108

In Kathmandu and Pokhara, ATMs are now common, but not always reliable. Bring some foreign cash in case of problems. Moneychangers are very quick to change cash, but travellers' cheques are no longer usable in Nepal. It's a waste of time to head for a bank these days, as most rarely exchange money and if they do are generally exceedingly slow. Currently there are no banks on the trails except in Lukla and Namche, with ATMs. In the hills, you may find a self-appointed moneychanger offering poor rates for cash. Take more cash rupees than you think you will need, and then a bit more.

Language

The main language of Nepal is Nepali, but many people also speak some English. It is taught in schools across the country and is understood to varying extents by all staff involved in tourism. The main ethnic groups also each have their own language. Everyone understands '*Namaste*' – hands held together, with a smile.

Internet and phone

A full range of internet-based services are available in Kathmandu and Pokhara. International dialling code: +977.

Mobile phones have completely changed the nature of 'getting away from it all' on holiday anywhere these days and in Nepal it is the same. It's no big deal these days to call anywhere across the globe from Everest Base Camp and even high up the peak! When disgruntled trekkers can call their travel agent at home to complain about the lack of hot water in their lodge, perhaps things have gone too far! However, foreign SIM cards may not work and, if they do, costs will be extortionate. With 3G and 4G networks in some parts of the country, trekkers who buy a local SIM card can become entangled in the worldwide web on their smartphones. But is that such a smart idea?

Nepal never really got past the first hurdle in developing landlines and thus avoided that vast investment. For a few brief years landline phones had great novelty value, with roughly one phone booth every four days' trekking distance. Nowadays people in the smallest village or trailside shack are busy keeping in touch with family down the valley. Monks seem very enamoured of phones, to keep in touch with the middle way perhaps! However, there are some corners of Nepal where mobile coverage is absent or erratic. Make sure your staff are carrying a charged satellite phone.

Postage

You'll need to trek into the old city to find the Central Post Office. To send a letter or postcard it's normally better to use your hotel or a bookshop. To send home heavy souvenirs, check out the packing agents in Thamel.

Electricity

Electricity in Nepal is 220volts/50cycles, with most sockets having two pins of varying distances apart. Electrification of the countryside is progressing well, but power cuts (load shedding) in cities can occur. In recent years hydroelectric schemes have been installed across many villages in the regions, but sadly some of those at higher altitude have frozen and not been repaired. Across the majority of the popular trekking regions, electricity is found in some form in most lodges. Charging your camera battery is possible in most but not all lodges – be sure to bring an electrical adaptor and more spare batteries than you expect to use.

National holidays

Sometimes there seem to be more official and unofficial holidays than there are normal days. As luck would have it, the busy trekking season in the autumn coincides with the biggest festival period. Enjoy the colourful festivities, but allow more time to get your permits.

National holidays

1 January	New Year
February/March	Tibetan New Year
14 April	Nepali New Year
23 April	Democracy Day
1 May	Labour Day
28 May	Republic Day

Plus many other religious festivals.
For comprehensive listings, see
www.qppstudio.net/publicholidays2019/nepal.htm

Trek planning

> I knew too well that a mountain journey is never a triumphant progression toward a shining goal, but rather a limited quest, a daily struggle to reach the village or campsite just ahead.
> ***Stones of Silence*, George Schaller**

Trek permits and TIMS

Trek permits of some form are necessary for most treks in Nepal. See www.timsnepal.com for the latest requirements. They are issued at the main office in the Bhrikuti Mandap tourist service centre.

There are two types of TIMS. The blue one is issued to trekkers organising the trek through a Nepalese trekking agency and costs US$10. The green TIMS card is issued to independent trekkers and costs US$20 per person.

In addition, some restricted areas require special permits that must be obtained from the Immigration Office by a registered trekking agency. Currently there are no special permits for most of the Dhaulagiri region unless straying into Dolpo. If anyone gets across the Ruwachaur Himal ridge they will need a TIMS card and ACAP permit (Rs2000 in Kathmandu and maybe double on arrival in Lete/Ghasa).

Peak permits

Peak permit fees are currently levied at various rates according to the classification and altitude of the peak. The list shown on the NMA website is only a sample. The major peaks are not listed and nor are many of the newly opened peaks. An additional 'garbage' deposit fee may be levied, refundable when the garbage is deposited at the registered depot for the particular climbing peak. Liaison officers are also sometimes required.

The Nepal Mountaineering Association (NMA) office is in Nag Pokhari near the Chinese Embassy. Check out the latest details, rules and fees at:

www.nepalmountaineering.org
Tel: +977-1-4434525, 4435442
Email: office@nepalmountaineering.org
peaks@nma.wlink.com.np
info@nepalmountaineering.org

National park entry fees

Visitors to many trekking regions are required to pay for entry to National Parks and Conservation Areas. The fees currently range from Rs2000–Rs3000 and the permits can be obtained in advance from the Bhrikuti Mandap tourist service centre in Kathmandu. It is also possible to pay at most of the park entry gates for those not sure of their plans in advance, but the fee is sometimes doubled.

National parks

The general aim of the national parks is to regulate activities and promote conservation. Prior to the formation of the national parks and conservation areas, there was fairly uncontrolled deforestation, since local people relied on the timber for cooking and heating. In association with local community development, the projects seek to develop ecological ways of improving the environment. Trekking groups are forbidden to use wood for cooking. Hygiene levels are being improved through the establishment of small health posts, toilets and safe drinking water depots. Bridges and basic infrastructure have been improved and new schools have opened. The preservation of the local culture has been another important contribution; evidence of this is seen through the restoration of key cultural monuments, such as the once-decaying monasteries.

Associated organisations
NTNC (National Trust for Nature Conservation)
www.ntnc.org.np; www.forestrynepal.org
TAAN (Trekking Agents' Association of Nepal)
www.taan.org.np
See also www.welcomenepal.com & www.tourism.gov.np

Important note

The **single entry** to any national park does mean just one entry. This means that if you leave one part of the park hoping to re-enter in another, you will be refused re-entry. This rule only affects trekkers where roads mean it's possible to shortcut some trails.

Choosing the season

Treks to most areas of Nepal are best undertaken in either autumn or spring. The autumn period is usually the most stable period and thus will be the busiest time on the trails. Normally early October heralded the beginning of the season after the monsoon rains abated, but in recent years the weather has sometimes been more unsettled. Unseasonal rain and heavy cloud has intervened, causing the much awaited and colourful harvests to be delayed.

After mid-October the weather is usually better, with clearer skies and magical views. The ripened rice terraced hillsides are ablaze with fabulous colours from gold to brilliant greens of all shades. November is generally the clearest month, with crisp and sparkling days. December is much colder at higher altitude, but trails are quieter. Just occasionally the stable conditions of autumn are disrupted when a storm blows in, bringing rain with heavy snow in the mountains.

Trekking throughout the winter is perfectly possible lower down, but heading to the higher valleys during late December/January and early February will mean encountering more cloud, snow and colder temperatures. Some inhabitants descend to the warmer foothills for winter, so occasionally accommodation may be closed. Heavy snow will make some higher and narrow trails dangerous if not impossible, with a risk of avalanche.

The spring season, late February to early May, is the other popular trekking season. The weather is generally stable, but clouds often cover the mountains by mid-morning. The lower valleys (below 2500m) are sultry and hot. Crossing high passes before April could be tricky, with snow and ice a serious deterrent. Haze will unfortunately mean those photographers who want their mountains crisp and clear might feel frustrated.

However, keen botanists are sure to be delighted and satisfied with the prolific array of rhododendrons and magnolia. Heading into the high country, wind tends to be more of a feature, particularly closer to the Tibetan plateau.

For most, trekking at the height of the summer, July and August, is not really recommended, with mountain vistas a rare luxury. Monsoon cloud, rain and snow can be expected at any time from mid-June to mid-September. Incessant rain in the lower hills causes dangerous landslides, road and trail damage. Blood-sucking leeches are a plague. The one positive advantage about a visit in the monsoon is that the valleys are green and the experience is totally different. The farmers are busy in the fields and some of the main festivals and colourful events are celebrated.

Areas that are commonly visited during the summer (monsoon) include Mustang and Dolpo, on the north side of the high mountains. However, the approaches are through the weather-affected and landslide-afflicted middle hills. These authors are wary of trekking anywhere during the monsoon season (being addicted to the views), but others relish the different atmosphere and the many festivals that are celebrated during that period.

Maps

> Frodo began to feel restless, and the old paths seemed too well-trodden. He looked at maps, and wondered what lay beyond their edges: maps made in the Shire showed mostly white spaces beyond its borders.
> ***The Lord of the Rings*, J R R Tolkien**

There is an amazing and varied number of maps available in Kathmandu. The quality has improved dramatically in recent years, with excellent colour maps showing all the aspects and features that any casual trekker to Nepal might wish for. Place names on maps are often spelt differently from those seen on lodge signs and so on. Most of the maps are produced by Himalayan Map House (www.himalayan-maphouse.com), who have a bookshop in Freak Street and opposite KC's restaurant in Thamel: the Map Centre. In Thamel there are a number of other map stockists, who also sell books on all aspects of the Himalaya.

A selection of titles is listed below:

Dhaulagiri Sanctuary	1: 60,000
Dhaulagiri Circuit	1: 90,000
Dhaulagiri & Kanjirowa	1: 265,000
West Dhaulagiri	1: 160,000
Gurja Himal & Hidden Village	1: 100,000
Guerrilla Trail	1: 60,000
Around Annapurna	1: 100,000
Upper & Lower Dolpo	1: 125,000
Dhorpatan Hunting Reserve	1: 150,000

In the UK, Stanfords in Long Acre, London is one of the best places to find maps of Nepal and the Himalaya. www.stanfords.co.uk

Photography

The Himalaya and anywhere in Nepal are a photographer's Shangri-La. The variety of the subject matter is mind-boggling. The mountains in all their aspects, the colourful people, the architecture and antiquities, bustling markets and every conceivable subject all offer wonderful opportunities. For much of the season the clarity of the mountain light is often brilliant. Keep all your photographic equipment in plastic bags, away from the unavoidable dust. Batteries do not like the sub-zero nights and need a warm up in the mornings just as much as the trekkers!

You may need to sleep with your camera/battery when temperatures drop at night; keep the camera tucked up close to your body inside a jacket to warm it up before use. Bring cleaning equipment. Be sure to buy all your film beforehand if you haven't gone digital, as it's virtually unavailable in Nepal now. Power supplies can be erratic, so pack extra batteries and memory cards.

Avoid taking photographs of any military-looking subjects, such as check posts, some bridges and communication towers. You are strongly urged to ask permission of people before taking photographs, especially in the remote areas, where they still believe it will upset their spirits or ancestors.

Yaks love having their photos taken, but not from a point blank range – watch those horns! If you manage to capture a snow leopard on digital, you'll probably be able to pay for your trek.

Budgeting

For full-service group trekkers there will be few extras other than a rare beer/drink at a lodge, the odd souvenirs, staff tips and meals out in Kathmandu. Independent trekkers need to obtain the TIMS and park entry fees and calculate the costs with much more care. They will need to plan for porters, camping crews and food, as well as the above extras.

Costs on trek
In general the higher you go, the higher the bills for food and accommodation. On the Dhaulagiri Sanctuary route the local village meal prices are still low. Expect Rs150–Rs250 for dal bhat. The exception we experienced was in Kotgaon, where dal bhat was Rs500 each for us and the crew! Plan on spending Rs1500–2000 per day for homestays. Elsewhere in the region allow Rs2500–3500 for lodging and 'fooding'. Higher up trekkers will need to allow Rs3500–Rs4000 per day (or more if having beer after the high points).

Organising your own guide and porters through a recognised trekking agent is perfectly feasible. Allow at least US$25–35 per day for a guide, $20–25 for a porter-guide and $15–20 for a porter. Be sure to confirm in advance whether or not these wages **also include** his or her expenses en route. Don't forget to have insurance for local staff.

Dal Bhat Index
Dal bhat is a good indicator of rising costs!

Kathmandu	Rs300–700
Beni	Rs200
Jhi	Rs150–200
Ghyasikharka	Rs250
Kalopani	Rs350–450
Ghorepani	Rs300–450
Marpha	Rs350–450

Take **more cash** than you have calculated, as there are few ATMs in the countryside nor are there many official places to change money. You don't want to spend all winter in a quaint but freezing gompa reciting prayers for deliverance! Expect prices to rise by up to 10 per cent or so a year in future.

Tipping

Since the 1960s, when trekking in Nepal was developed, there has been a tradition for groups and independent visitors to tip their crews at the end of a trek. It's no great hardship to budget for this and it's very rare that anyone is dissatisfied with the service. As a rule and through tradition, the head cook should get a little more than the porters, 'sherpas' and kitchen crews. The sirdar and leader/guide would expect a little more again. Allow around 15% per cent of the wages or around one day's wage for each week on trek. Trekkers may also wish to donate some of their clothing and equipment to the crew.

Style of trekking

Trekkers will find good facilities across the Annapurna region, but more limited as yet in the adjacent Dhaulagiri area. Most trekking trails traditionally connected the villages and very little of Nepal is true wilderness. The trails of the higher regions are generally less populated, apart from the occasional lost yak or yeti. However, the middle hills can be quite busy with local porters, people off to markets, children engaging visitors, wary dogs, banana-snatching monkeys, mad cows and 'mad' trekkers as well as mules and dzopkios.

As much as anything, the itinerary you choose and the destination will dictate the style of trek undertaken. The following section outlines the trekking style options.

Independent trekking

Across many of the more frequented trekking areas of Nepal, going independently is quite easy. Those fit and able to carry their own equipment often choose this style of trek. It is a very popular option on the main trails. Elsewhere expect a few very basic places and be prepared to camp.

> **Trekkers Beware**
> A typical sign at a lodge in Nepal, relevant to most wild areas, reads:
>
> "Although (this) National Park is open for single trekker, remoteness, altitude sickness, inadequate lodge facilities cause trekkers to fall into unhappy events." And in addition take note of the following: "It is unsafe to trekking singly because undesirable events like tourist lost, and indulgent into accident have been reported for some years."

There are a few downsides to the independent format, of course. That backpack always seems to get heavier throughout the day, especially on all those dastardly steep hills. That is why taking a porter makes such an appealing difference on a hard and demanding trek.

Although adding to the cost of the trek, having a guide or porter-guide makes any trek easier and generally safer. Many routes are exposed, rough and deserted for long periods. The higher passes have no emergency facilities and any accident up there could have very serious consequences. A good guide can impart a lot of local knowledge, act as a translator and generally make a trek a memorable experience. Of course having a less-than-amiable guide can make a trek less enjoyable in many ways. Fortunately there are few guides with an attitude problem.

Going independently does allow for perhaps greater interaction and a very intimate rapport with the inhabitants. It is also a cheaper way to trek in Nepal and ensures that your cash goes straight to the local people. Those who have already been to Nepal or other developing countries will have the added advantage of knowing roughly what to expect.

Independently organised trips

Those trekkers who have a dislike for organised trips will find this an appealing option. It offers a good deal of freedom and flexibility. The trek can be tailored to the needs of the person, couple or small group of friends.

Many trekkers hire a local porter/guide through a reputable agency, paying all their living expenses as well as the wage.

This approach can easily be applied to any trekking region. It doesn't make a lot of sense to hire only a guide, since the extra cost of the porter(s) is not a significant amount on top of all the permits and park fees. That said, it's perfectly permissible to take a guide only and carry all your own gear. Make sure that the guide, porters and any staff are insured and adequately clothed for the high altitude. Make sure also that the agency will cover any additional porter insurance if your bag is too heavy and you hire an extra porter on the way.

Hiring porters off the street and hotel areas is not necessarily a good idea these days, unless it comes through reliable recommendation. **Be sure to read the sections in this guide on altitude and mountain safety.** The points may seem obvious, but every year people are evacuated from or die in these mountains.

Organising a trip through an agent in your home country or Nepal for a couple or a small group is not necessarily more expensive than a big company group trek. Naturally, booking the trek directly with a Kathmandu-based company is cheaper. However, unless you are familiar with the agency or have a recommendation, there may be snags. The main one is that you will not be covered by any foreign company liability if things do go badly. At the very least make sure your insurance covers a helicopter evacuation and is not limited by absurd altitude limits such as 'not above 1500m'.

There is a good selection of excellent local trekking agents in Kathmandu who have years of experience in dealing with overseas trekkers approaching them directly. Sometimes getting an answer to your enquiry quickly does not happen because of the fickle nature of power cuts experienced in Kathmandu these days – just keep on asking. Choosing to arrange the trip with a Kathmandu agent means you can finalise the trip and pay the operators directly, but remember that if an internal flight is involved, the agent might ask for some advance payment.

An Independent trekker's day

Independent trekkers have the option of a luxurious lie-in, making all those group members envious. Invariably, though, you will be up, up and away at the same time as the early birds, catching the dawn chorus, with the first rays glinting on that fabulous peak outside. After breakfast the day is much the same for all, except that you can dictate your own pace, itinerary and lunch spots.

Fully supported group treks

For many years this was the only option (until guidebook writers came up with notes on the main trails!). For those with limited time, this option provides maximum security and the least amount of hassle getting permits, for example, in Kathmandu. The tour operators can smooth over the local difficulties and sort out any issues like transport, permits and porter strikes!

The big companies (foreign and Nepalese) can also organise any private helicopters or rescues more easily. The agent will arrange the trekking permits and conservation fees. All day-to-day logistics such as accommodation, food and carriage of baggage will be arranged. Most trips are fully inclusive, with few added extras. Clients can admire the scenery in as much comfort as is possible in a high mountain environment. Group treks invariably now utilise lodges wherever available, instead of camping.

There are a few disadvantages to commercial group trekking. Larger groups with the support of a Nepali crew can have more of an impact on the environment. Sometimes clients have to wait at a lodge or campground for the porters to arrive. The major disadvantage of an organised trek is that there is a loss of flexibility concerning the itinerary and any other issues. Of course there is always the risk that your fellow trekkers are on a different planet – although this is extremely rare. Perhaps the biggest snag of a group trek is the unnecessary danger posed at altitude by 'peer pressure' within the group. No one wants to be 'tail-end Charlie' or the first to admit to a headache or nauseas.

At its worst, this pressure can overrule common sense, with some members ignoring symptoms of altitude sickness in the unacknowledged race to compete. **Do not fall into this lethal trap**.

A typical group trekker's day
Fully supported hikers can expect a mug of steaming hot tea thrust through their tent at dawn, around 6am. This is the wake-up call to 'get up now and pack your bags'. During breakfast, the porter loads will be organised and home sweet home – the tents – will be dismantled. Those who actually found a lodge can luxuriate in a warm sleeping bag for longer but may set off a little hungry.

No sooner is breakfast over and the loads packed, then it's on with the trekking – be sure to use the loo (toilet) in the lodge before heading out! Normally the longer walks during the day are before lunch, to luxuriate in the cool, refreshing air and the clarity of the mountain views. Generally the pre-lunch hikes last 3–4hrs, including the odd tea stop along the way where possible. Lunch is taken at a convenient spot en route, often prearranged if it's a big group. Lunch might be spring rolls, spaghetti cheese, noodles or even dal bhat. Desert may include a pancake, apple pie slice or a banana fritter, all washed down by gallons of tea or even lukewarm milk coffee – yuk! Some you win, some you lose!

Most of the afternoon walks are around 3hrs, with some less and some more depending on the terrain. Trekkers have no need to outperform the guides, or they might end up in the wrong village. After unpacking and setting out the sleeping bags there is time to read, check the itinerary notes – oops – rest or explore the locality. As the light fades, those who enjoy a beer might have to become teetotal or risk a tipple of the local brews – although this is not recommended at the beginning of any hard trek due to the dubious quality control of the liquor. It's wise to avoid alcohol of any description before any high pass or high terrain, since it adversely affects acclimatisation. A dinner of delightful goodies is served piping hot a little after sunset. Then the day is done, except for crawling into that uncooperative sleeping bag.

Guides and porters

Group trekkers will be led by an English-speaking Nepalese leader/guide who normally knows the routes. Other crew are the sherpas, which in this context refers to the job of guiding the group on the trail. They keep track of wayward trekkers lingering in the forest watching for red pandas or sneaking off ahead. The porters for a large group might number 30–40. In that case there will also be a *naiki* – a head porter, who takes some of the responsibilities from the sirdar, organising and distributing the loads. The naiki has a hard job deciding who carries the tricky loads, like the eggs or the kerosene, and watching for that 'wily old fox', who unloads his heavy items on to another porter.

As mentioned before but reiterated here, independent trekkers hiring a crew or a porter locally or from Kathmandu should ensure that insurance is obtained to cover any misadventure involving the guide/porters. They should also ensure that suitable clothing is provided for all guides/porters for the high altitude. Check out KEEP for guidance on the correct actions when hiring porters or guides privately.

Porter welfare

Being a porter is a hard and often dangerous way to make a living in the hill country of Nepal. Every year a few porters are killed through accidents on the trails of Nepal, and occasionally some of them are in the employ of foreign trekkers. Fortunately today there is much more awareness of the conditions once endured by porters. Exploitation has always been found in most societies, but in Nepal the theoretically outlawed caste system, which still pervades the roots of its culture, ensures the situation is very complex. However, visitors can avoid such attitudes. Following the Maoist insurgency, general wage levels for porters and many other often poorly treated people throughout society have risen dramatically – perhaps the one benefit of that long reign of violence!

The International Porter Protection Group and Tourism Concern have both made an impact on porter welfare. All trekking agencies in Nepal are now required to provide adequate insurance and clothing for all their staff.

> **ABC Porter guidelines for all trekkers:**
> **A** Always ensure that your porters have adequate clothing and equipment for the level of trek you are undertaking: footwear, hat, gloves, warm clothing and sleeping bags or blankets as necessary.
> **B** Be prepared with extra medicines for your porters, and don't abandon them if they are sick; carry funds for such a situation.
> **C** Choose a local or foreign trekking company who implement the ethical practices outlined above and keep an eye on the reality on the ground.

Accommodation

Lodges

Lodges are plentiful and relatively comfortable across the Annapurna area but not along the trails of Dhaulagiri. Lodges generally have small but adequate twin-bedded rooms. Beds tend to be fairly hard, and the dividing walls hardly provide a private boudoir – expect a lot of communal interaction. Mattresses are getting thicker each year, so very few trekkers need bother to carry a Thermarest. As the Annapurna region becomes ever more cosmopolitan, with trekkers from every corner of the globe, the choice of accommodation is blossoming. Today it's possible to trek here while staying in some very well-appointed accommodation.

Overnight charges range from Rs200–Rs500 and then US$80+ per person for the luxury Ker and Downey Lodges in the Modi Khola valley.

There are no regular lodges in the rest of the Dhaulagiri area, only people's houses with a spare room or two.

At the start of the Dhaulagiri Circuit a few basic lodges are available in the lower reaches. Across the Gurja Himal area, homestay is the normal option, plus camping. Higher up it's all camping until Marpha. In the Dhaulagiri-Dolpo area there are a few basic lodges. Homestay and basic houses are found, but again most of the trekking route needs camping.

Camping
Not so many trekkers camp these days in the Annapurna area but for most of the Dhaulagiri treks camping remains the main option. Group camping trekkers can expect quite a degree of comfort in often wild, remote regions. On a traditional camping trek, large two-man tents are used and a mess tent is provided to act as a dining room and porter shelter when necessary. In addition, dining tables, chairs, toilet tents and mattresses come as standard. A wide variety of food is provided and cooked by the crews.

Homestay
Homestay is a new but essentially old concept, where trekkers overnight in local people's houses. Normally a separate room is set aside for guests. Most homestays are basic, with outside toilets and primitive washing facilities – much as the first trekkers found. Mattresses may be thin or even thinner! Meals are provided by the household, using any available local produce. Nourishing dal bhat (lentils and rice) and potatoes are commonly available. Delicious, local organic vegetables are sometimes on offer.

Homestay in Chimkhola

Homestay and more primitive house-stay are found on the Dhaulagiri Sanctuary Trek and Gurja Himal. The Parbat Myagdi area treks have better facilities.

Washing

> How can we be out of soap? Judging by appearances, we have not been contaminated by soap for weeks.
> ***Stones of Silence*, George Schaller**

The Annapurna region is pretty developed these days, so washing there is less of an issue. However, in the Dhaulagiri area things are still much as they used to be. There are very few showers. You may be able to request a bucket of hot water, but heating the water might be ecologically unfriendly. With solar-heated water, most shower facilities do not now conflict with the use of scarce resources. Camping group trekkers receive a bowl of hot water in the mornings before breakfast, and sometimes on arrival at camp as well.

Toilets

It's a certain bet that the subject of toilets is being discussed at any time, almost anywhere on trek across Nepal. In the more developed parts, lodges will have western-style toilets, sometimes even en suite. However, at higher altitudes the water freezes overnight, making the outside shed full of sawdust a more appealing option! Elsewhere, toilets are outside, invariably up or down (or both) small, steep slopes or steps. Group campers will be privileged with a special toilet tent with appropriate hole – they're better than nothing! A trekker's worst nightmare is dropping their moneybelt down the hole, so be extra vigilant. Along the trails, toilet paper should be burnt and waste buried where possible.

> We have discovered, as have Tibetans long ago, that the luxury of warmth far outweighs that of cleanliness.
> ***Stones of Silence*, George Schaller**

Food

Most treks to Dhaulagiri require taking all or most food. Those on fully inclusive group or independently organised treks with full services will enjoy filling breakfasts, including porridge/cereal, bread/toast with eggs, plus hot drinks. Lunch is a favourite meal, especially the real chips. Other items are likely to be tinned meat/fish, noodles or cooked bread and something sweet to round off. At night campers are provided with three-course dinners: soup, noodles/pasta/rice/potatoes plus a dessert of tinned fruit Plentiful amounts of hot water/drinks are available at all meal times to ensure dehydration is avoided, especially the higher you trek. As a rule, food prices increase the further you get from Kathmandu, as the fresh products are more limited. However, by now anything tastes good!

Kathmandu has a good variety of supermarkets, but don't anticipate many treats elsewhere. New city malls are the latest trend in Kathmandu, with imported food items suitable for trekkers. Be sure to stock up on goodies – chocolate or power bars and any other cravings that need to be satisfied en route. There's not much on offer in the small shops unless you like chewing tobacco and rough cigarettes!

'Fried chaps'

The Nepalis' use of the English language is one of the most endearing features of the country. You'll see this on signboards advertising the lodges' 'faxsilities', such as inside 'to lets', 'toilet free rooms' and, on enticing teahouse menus, 'fried chaps', 'apple panick', 'banana crap', 'pumping soup', 'chocolate putting', 'palin chapatti', 'spleeping charge' and the like. Flash toilets invariably mean toilets flushed by water (or ice blocks) and it is a notorious fact that toilets and Nepal are not cuddly bedfellows.

When trekking for a long period anywhere in Nepal and living in the teahouses, the food can eventually get rather monotonous. It's worthwhile taking other food items if you have a porter or two. Muesli is a good standby for any time of day – even with water. Instant potato, soups or noodles and tinned fish are easily prepared as an emergency dinner at a high camp. Ensure that indestructible rubbish is carried out, or use the places set aside for disposal.

What to take

Some of the equipment listed below will involve a considerable expense when purchased at home. Some commercial trekking companies do now provide basic gear – sleeping bags, mattresses etc – but others do not. A few trekking gear shops in Kathmandu offer equipment for hire quite cheaply. Buying new gear is also good value, with excellent locally made items like sleeping bags and down jackets – Mingmar at the Everest Equipment shop (near the Kathmandu Guest House) has such items. We have been buying boots in Kathmandu for a number of years and most have proved quite durable. Boots can cost as little as US$50.

The following kit list is a guideline only:	
Kitbag	Walking poles
Torch (flashlight) & whistle	Trainers or sandals
Washing kit	Fleece and woollen hat
Wetwipes, large and small	Sunglasses & sun hat
Toothbrush & toothpaste	Gloves and scarf/buff
Sun cream & lip cream	Waterproof jacket/trousers
Water bottle	Warm sweater
Trousers or cotton skirts	Down jacket/trousers
Shirts, T-shirts or blouses	Penknife and tin opener
Underwear	Padlock for cheap hotel rooms
Boots and various socks	
Sleeping bag + fleece liner	Ear plugs
Toilet rolls	Camera & batteries
Plastic bags	Adaptor for electric plugs

The motto for mountain and wilderness trekkers and visitors around the world is:

Leave only footprints and take only photographs

Staying healthy

The main problems concerning health issues in Nepal are related to food, water, hygiene, the remoteness of the trekking regions, and the high altitude. Outside the main centres of Kathmandu and Pokhara, it cannot be emphasised enough that there are virtually no adequate medical facilities anywhere other than tiny, often barely functioning, health posts.

However, helicopter evacuations are possible from some parts of the mountain regions. You must have proof of medical evacuation insurance or payment before a helicopter will take off. (Helicopter quotes range from US$1600 per hour up to a whopping US$10,000, which might include a 'booking fee'.)

In general fewer bugs survive at high altitude, making the high zones of Nepal marginally healthier than the humid lowland destinations – a small comfort at least. Personal hygiene and what you eat really does matter. Unfortunately some local levels of hygiene still leave a lot to be desired by most standards.

> **Do your best to keep healthy:**
> Wash/clean hands regularly
> Never drink untreated tap water
> Avoid salads
> Peel fruits
> Brush teeth in bottled/cleaned water

Water sterilisation

Many difficulties on trek concern the lack of clean running water. Just keeping your hands clean can significantly reduce the ailments transmitted through dirty water. The lodges and homestays on the trails are slowly becoming more aware of hygiene these days. Group trekkers are at a distinct advantage, being regularly supplied with plentiful boiled water and hot drinks. Independent trekkers will need to be more vigilant as a rule. Antibacterial gel for hands and large baby wipes for other parts are extremely useful! Bring plastic bags for storing used items and carry out rubbish.

Water boils at a lower temperature at high altitude, so you might want to add sterilising tablets to the water as an added precaution. Iodine or chlorine tablets, or Micropur, can be used. Bottled drinking water can also be bought in Kathmandu and Pokhara. Along the trails, when available, it gets very expensive, especially the higher you go. Plastic water bottles have littered trails in the past but these days most are being carried out of the mountains by trekkers and crews. However, plastic pollution is becoming more and more of an issue worldwide, so we do not recommend it. A better option for independent hikers is to request boiled water from the lodges. Other options include bottles from www.watertogo.eu

Vaccinations

At present no vaccinations are legally required on entry to Nepal, but always check before travel in case of any recent changes. Your GP can advise you about the latest recommendations regarding vaccinations.

Be sure to allow plenty of time for the series of vaccinations – they cannot all be given at the same time and some require a number of weeks in-between. Keep a record of all the vaccinations, even though it's not a legal requirement.

The following are normally recommended by health professionals, but there could be others added at any time.

BCG tuberculosis Vaccination is often recommended by GPs.
Cholera Although not required by law or particularly effective, it might be recommended if an outbreak has occurred.
Hepatitis This nasty disease has various forms; hepatitis A is the main risk for travellers. New vaccines are being improved for all strains of hepatitis.
Meningitis/Japanese encephalitis Outbreaks do occur in rural parts of Nepal, often in the lower country. The risk is minimal and expensive vaccines are available. Clinics in Kathmandu can give vaccinations for a much lower negotiable fee than payable at home; the CIWEC clinic is highly recommended.
Rabies The disease is found across Nepal, but the vaccine is normally only suggested for those spending extended periods in rural areas away from the cities. The vaccination is expensive and the procedure lengthy, but it should be considered for remote areas of Nepal. Seek advice at least six months before the planned trip. The main thing for casual visitors is to keep a sharp lookout for suspiciously acting dogs and 'dog patrols.'

Although not necessarily a risk for rabies, the guard dogs of herders in the high uplands can be rather intimidating and occasionally menacing if the owners are not present. A few monasteries have guard dogs, so beware!
Tetanus/polio Recommended.
Typhoid/paratyphoid Vaccinations are strongly recommended, as there are possible risks.
Yellow fever Vaccination will give cover for 10 years. It is only required in Nepal if coming from an infected area.

Other nasty bugs
Giardia is a wretched bug to watch out for, since there is no preventative treatment apart from careful eating and drinking. Infected drinking water is the main culprit. Giardia lives happily in its host until sent packing by a course of Flagyl (Metronidazole), Secnidazole or Tinidazole (Tiniba in Nepal). Sulphurous foul-smelling gases, cramp and sometimes diarrhoea are the main symptoms, but let's not dwell on those.

Dengue fever outbreaks are sometimes reported in Nepal, but the risk is generally fairly low. Try to avoid mosquito bites, since there is no treatment other than rest.

Malaria
Fortunately malaria is not found in most of Nepal, being confined at the moment to parts of the southern lowlands bordering India. However, those trekkers travelling overland to India, or relaxing in Chitwan National Park, or anywhere in the Terai, will be exposed to malaria. Using insect repellent at and after dusk and wearing suitable clothing will give some protection against bites. The three main drugs used in Nepal are Mefloquine (Lariam), Doxycycline and Malarone (Atovaquone/proguanil). For some users, Lariam can have very nasty side effects, so it is wise to test it out before travel. Some travellers may be recommended to take Proguanil daily and Chloroquine weekly, if going to a high-risk area. Doxycycline can be bought in Kathmandu if you need supplies. Do not ignore the risks of malaria.
See also www.masta-travel-health.com and
www.ciwec-clinic.com/articles/malaria_advice.php

Common ailments on trek

The most common problems on trek are colds, blocked sinuses, headaches and stomach disorders. Common remedies (available from the chemist) for headaches, blocked noses, sore throats, coughs and sneezes should be easily accessible in any medical kit. The dry air often causes irritations. Take a good supply of decongestants and painkillers for headaches on any high altitude trek. It is necessary to drink more liquids in high dry regions. If the dreaded stomach bug appears, the use of Imodium, Loperamide or Lomotil is initially recommended if symptoms are not serious. These drugs will make a road journey much more comfortable. The antibiotic drugs Norfloxacin and Ciprofloxacin can be used in more debilitating cases, and are available from pharmacies in Kathmandu. Dioralyte will help rehydration in cases of fluid loss due to stomach upsets. Stemetil can be used for those prone to travel sickness.

It may seem obvious, but don't ignore the power of the sun at high altitude, despite the low temperatures; wear a suitable hat and cover your arms and legs; use sun cream on exposed parts of the body.

Lipstick
Add a touch of glamour and protect your lips at the same time! For many years I simply used colourless lip protector sticks, but returned from Dolpo with a horribly cracked lower lip despite frequent use. Since then I have worn a standard coloured moisturising lipstick... and it works!

Dental care

> A day may come when the courage of men fails... but it is not THIS day.
> ***The Lord of the Rings*, J R R Tolkien**

A visit to your dentist for a check-up before the trip is advised (unless you wish to rely on the 'tooth temple god' near Tahity Square in Kathmandu for treatment). Competent dentists do exist in Kathmandu, but you are unlikely to meet any serving time in the hills. If the 'tooth god' has failed you, try Healthy

Smiles in Lazimpat in Kathmandu – it has the latest high-tech gadgetry.

Clinics

Consult one of the specialist clinics or their websites listed below for the latest medical advice for travellers. Your doctor should also be consulted.

CIWEC Clinic Lainchaur, near the British Embassy in Kathmandu, www.ciwec-clinic.com
International Society of Travel Medicine www.istm.org
Hospital for Tropical Diseases Travel Clinic www.thehtd.org
MASTA (Medical Advisory Service for Travellers Abroad) www.masta-travel-health.com.

First aid kit

The following list is only given as a suggestion:

Antibacterial hand gel	Insect repellent
Antibiotics (general)	Knee bandage
Antihistamine cream	Safety pins
Antiseptic cream	Scissors
Aspirin/paracetamol	Sterile gloves
Blister prevention	Sun cream
Rehydration sachets	Thermometer
Dressings	Water sterilising tablets
Eyewash	Wet wipes

Plus: Pocket First Aid and Wilderness Medicine Dr Jim Duff and Dr Peter Gormly (Cicerone)
Cold and sinus remedies
Personal medications
Stomach upset remedies and Tinidazole

If this lot fails to sort you out, check out the local remedies.

RISK: Remember altItude Sickness Kills

Descending is the only safe cure, day or night!

Altitude sickness & precautions

All mountain walking presents hazards, but in the high regions the biggest danger comes from the dehydrating high altitude, severe cold and bitter winds. Be careful on the rough and rocky trails; bear in mind that the next hospital is miles away. The real problems of altitude sickness occur at heights above 3000m (10,000ft), especially if you climb quickly.

There are generally two levels where the effects of altitude kicks in, 3500m and again around 4500m, so these two stages of upward motion should be carefully planned. Even before you reach 3000m, it is beneficial to gain height as slowly as possible, including extra nights. The recommended daily height gain is only 300m, with 500m per day being the upper limit. Obviously in some areas this is difficult, so you must monitor your condition closely.

Serious altitude problems occur in the highest mountain regions of northern Nepal. Kathmandu is at 1317m and presents no problems. To combat the problems of altitude, it is important to learn about its effects before you start hiking along the trails. The most common symptoms of altitude are headaches, nausea, tiredness, lack of appetite and disorientation. It is often difficult to sleep and breathing becomes erratic (Cheyne-Stokes breathing). The heart might thump a bit disconcertingly at times. Be very careful not to overexert on arrival at any destination; symptoms often only begin to appear after an hour or more. Having some of these does not mean abandoning the trek, but watch out for any changes as altitude is gained. Mild symptoms, perhaps just a slight headache, are acceptable so long as they do not get worse or persist all day and night. One real nuisance is the need to urinate more, especially at night at a high camp, but it's a good sign as a rule!

It is vital to walk very slowly at altitude, especially when climbing any hill. If in doubt, be sure to admit any problems and don't be pressured by your fellow trekkers. Altitude sickness does kill. If you are having any serious effects before a high pass, it might require another intermediate night or at worst an immediate return downhill. Minor effects of altitude above 4500m are felt by most – nausea and extreme lethargy

– but symptoms will improve on the descent. Continuing to ascend with any persistent symptoms can lead to the serious risk of Pulmonary and Cerebral Oedema or even death. Deaths occur each year in the Himalaya and Nepal, despite all the warnings. Complications from altitude sickness can strike very quickly.

As an aid before the trek, some start a course of Diamox (Acetazolamide), a diuretic which thins the blood, making you urinate more – which is generally considered good at altitude. It can have the disturbing side effect of pins and needles in the fingers. Another option is to try homeopathic coca, a version of the substance used by natives of Peru and Bolivia. Coca is available as homeopathic tablets that some trekkers (including the authors) swear by. Others swear by ginkgo biloba tablets, which appear to work for unfathomable reasons. It is suggested that these can be taken twice a day for five days before arrival and one tablet a day during the trek. However, there are some side effects when taken with some prescription drugs and other substances so check with your GP.

Gamow bag and oxygen cylinders

A Gamow bag is a large bag used to temporarily relieve the effects of high altitude. An ill person with serious altitude problems can be cocooned under higher air pressure for a limited period to mimic a lower altitude. Oxygen cylinders are quite common in the Everest region but they are not commonly used by trekkers. Generally it's better to proceed slowly and try to avoid any problems.

Mountain safety

> Man has pondered the transience of existence since he became man, yet such reflections recur in high and lonely places.
> ***Stones of Silence***, **George Schaller**

It's not just the altitude that trekkers need to watch out for; all mountain walking presents hazards. In Nepal, apart from the high altitude, severe cold and bitter winds are another menace to guard against. Just after sun up, be sure to keep well wrapped up and during any day always carry enough warm clothing. This is particularly important to group trekkers, who will not have access to their portered baggage – having only their daysack.

In the deep gorges the sunlight disappears early in the afternoon (sometimes as early as 2.30pm) and temperatures plummet. Breathing through a scarf at high altitudes can help to retain fluids, and will help protect against dust and icy winds. The high passes can sometimes be notorious for deathly cold winds.

Unnoticed dehydration is easily overlooked; you may not necessarily feel like drinking – remember that tea and coffee are both diuretics, so keep vital fluids up. Electrolyte powders can be added to clean water if lethargy arises (apart from when going up steep trails, when a little tiredness can easily be explained!). Noting the colour of your urine is one good way to be aware of dehydration. If it's very yellow, you are not drinking enough. Always concentrate and take care on the trails – the nearest hospital is just a distant dream. At high altitudes you may not be thinking as clearly as normal. Leaping carelessly across streams, boulders or log bridges is an easy way to fall foul of snags.

Remember too that evacuation by helicopter is not guaranteed: you might be too high, there could be bad weather or there might easily be no serviceable helicopter in Pokhara or Kathmandu. Porters with cut-out baskets on their backs and ponies do occasionally carry out trekkers in an emergency. To avoid this rollercoaster ride, it's best not to fall over! As mentioned above, unruly dogs in Nepal are a less obvious menace. Normally these dogs are docile and easily controlled. However, during a night-time visit to the toilet, watch out! Ideally, plan on not going out at night at all, but improvise some sort of suitable receptacle. Find a large-necked plastic container and make sure the lid seal is good!

Of course there is no need to be put off by all the above advice; just take care and enjoy the trek!

Weather
No man or woman yet, including trekkers and climbers, has tamed the weather. However, today there are some high-tech

sages who can predict, with surprising accuracy, the weather patterns to come. Perhaps the gods will be on your side, but as a trekker it's not normally of so much consequence. However, for mountaineers and those heading for trekking peaks, other measures are possible to guard against unexpected storms.

> ### The Sorcerer of the Clouds
> Who is this modern-day high-tech, 'Sorcerer of the Clouds'? What can he do to weave his magical spell over the Himalaya? The mountaineer has one aim – to get to the top. However, skill alone cannot guarantee success; modern equipment, better protection against the biting cold, better food, oxygen and all manner of tools can enhance the chances of reaching the summit. Their destiny is also controlled by the clouds – well, the gods at least. Early 1920s climbers on Everest argued incessantly about the ethics of using of oxygen. Was it sporting?
>
> A new aid to the mountaineer is that of the 'router'. They are meteorologists, invariably of great dedication and skill, using real time, space age satellite imagery and superb communications to advise climbers about the prevailing weather conditions anywhere in the world. Incredibly accurate predictions and detailed information about wind speed and direction, cloud conditions and imminent changes in the weather can be obtained. Today 'The Sorcerer of the Clouds' can wave his wand to aid both safety and the chances of success on the peak, yet it is still ultimately the gods who cast the final spell.
>
> Yan Giezendanner is one such sorcerer who has 'climbed' the Himalaya through this meteorological technology without setting foot on any slope: he has done this from his wheelchair in Chamonix. A French book, *Le Routeur des Cimes* (Editions Guérin), tells his extraordinary story. It has been translated into English by Siân as *The Sorcerer of the Clouds* (Pilgrims).

Security

Once upon a time, as the fairytale goes, there was virtually no crime in Nepal, but those days have long gone. However, it is still an amazingly safe country for foreigners to visit. It is unlikely that anyone will encounter any danger in Kathmandu, even well into the night (though night owls might want to avoid grungy dogs in the early hours). Embassies and the tourist departments do not recommend trekking completely alone. You are strongly encouraged to register your trip at your embassy. Isolated incidents and attacks have occurred in the hills, and tent theft has increased. Take the usual, sensible precautions that you would observe almost anywhere these days.

Kathmandu – gateway to the Himalaya

Kathmandu (1317m) is the normal gateway to all parts of the Nepal Himalaya. Trekkers should spend a few days exploring the magical parts of the city. It's a friendly, welcoming place, despite some obvious distractions. The longer you stay, the more of a home away from home it becomes. There is a wide range of excellent hotels and guesthouses to suit all tastes and an astonishing array of eateries and restaurants. Despite the obvious modernisation, the city and the whole valley still have some enchanting places to discover.

Kathmandu Durbar Square

The Kathmandu Valley probably has the greatest concentration of temples, shrines, monasteries and idols of anywhere across the globe. Kathmandu is the trading crossroads of the Himalaya between India and China, through Tibet.

The city is a great melting pot of migrating peoples. The religious mix of Hinduism, Buddhism, Tantra, Vajrayana, Tibetan Buddhism, Bon and Shamanism is intoxicating. Legends, folktales and myths influence every Nepalese ritual and festival, as well as everyday actions. Idols once outnumbered people, but that is not quite the case today, although they do still outnumber tourists.

No visit to Nepal would be complete without a thorough exploration of the **Durbar (palace) squares** of the three great cities, Kathmandu, Patan and Bhaktapur. In Kathmandu, be sure to investigate the Jochen Tole alley also known as **Freak Street**. It's still there, bearing a faded resemblance to its glorious past. Those 'idle' hippies were the eccentric pioneers of Nepal's tourist industry. The bustling byways of **Asan**, Kathmandu's old market streets, are a kaleidoscope of colour and confusion. Brass pots, fabrics, metal and woodwork crafts and everyday items almost block the narrow lanes.

In Asan area is the **Jan Bahal**, a fairyland of glittering temples and devotional artwork. The enigmatic Seto (White) Machhendranath idol with the strangest mesmerising eyes resides here, surrounded by goldleaf. **Itum Bahal** is a typical Newari courtyard housing complex, hidden in a maze of dark mysterious alleyways close to Durbar Square; finding it is quite a mystery as well. **Sano (Little) Swayambhunath** and the temple of **Nara Devi** lie north of Durbar Square. To the south, down a small street from the Kasthamandap temple, are a number of tiered temples, like **Jaisi Dewal** and other shrines or stupas set in quiet courtyards – bahals.

Patan is a city of artisans and quaint, quiet lanes. The Durbar Square here is perhaps the most exotic of the three such squares of the valley and the number of impressive temples and palaces merely adds to this dimension. Deep in the old quarter are the **Kwa Bahal** (Golden Temple) and the temple of Rato (Red) Machhendranath, plus many other exquisite temples and shrines.

Patan Durbar Square

Bhaktapur, 11km east of Kathmandu, is the least modernised city of the valley, although a new multi-lane highway makes the journey there less of a Himalayan expedition today. Its **Durbar Square** is intriguing, with some impressive restoration after various earthquakes destroyed the once vast complex. Be sure not to miss the other squares.

Bhaktapur Durbar Square

Nyatapola Square displays a five-tiered temple and topsy-turvy temple cafe. **Dattatreya Square**, some distance to the east, magnificently illustrates the fabulous artistry and skill of the Malla-era builders. The whole scene is of overwhelming grandeur, with intricately carved wooden windows and fine brick structures. In the quiet mediaeval streets of Bhaktapur, time stands still – it's a living relic of a forgotten era.

On a hill to the west of Kathmandu is **Swayambhunath** (the Monkey Temple), a picturesque Buddhist stupa surrounded by shrines and temples. It's quite a climb up, but the views are stunning – it's a good workout for the trek to come. The great stupa of **Boudhanath**, with its all-seeing eyes and peaceful atmosphere, is east of Kathmandu. Pilgrims, monks, Tibetans and tourists circle the base in a clockwise direction, turning the prayer wheels, breathing the sweet aroma of juniper incense and enjoying the relaxing atmosphere.

Close to Boudhanath is the great Hindu temple complex of **Pashupatinath** beside the holy Bagmati River. Non-Hindu foreigners cannot enter the main shrine, where stands the great golden bull of Nandi – Shiva's vehicle. Across the river in a forested monkey-infested area, sadhus congregate and show a few surprising tricks. Along the riverbanks is a more sobering sight, where Hindus are cremated before passage into the next life.

'There's a green-eyed yellow idol to the north of Kathmandu' (so says the famous poem), but today only an image of Vishnu covered in snakes and reclining in a pool can be found – at **Budhanilkanta**.

Further afield in the valley to the south of Patan are **Bungamati** (with a quaint square hosting the Red Machhendranath temple) and **Kokhana** (with old brick houses and the Shekali Mai temple). Southwest of Patan are **Pharping** (Buddhist monasteries and Guru Rinpoche cave), **Shesh Narayan** (a temple devoted to Vishnu) and **Dakshinkali** (where pilgrims offer live sacrifices to the bloodthirsty goddess Kali).

If you have plenty of time, why not seek out other enchanting places: **Changu Narayan, Kirtipur, Vajra Yogini** near

Sankhu, the boar-headed Vajra Varahi temple garden of **Chapagaon**, quirky Bishankhu Narayan and the mountain viewpoints of **Nagarkot** and **Kakani**. A few kilometres to the east along the road to Tibet are **Dhulikhel**, **Panauti** and **Banepa**, with some little-visited temples and shrines.

Accommodation

The main Kathmandu tourist enclave for hotels and restaurants is Thamel, with rooms to suit most pockets. However, the fast-regenerating Freak Street should not be disregarded, with much lower prices. Our new home, the Hotel Moonlight, is in Paknajol near Thamel; Pilgrims Hotel is nearby through a small alleyway. The famous Kathmandu Guest House, originally the backpackers' favourite, was damaged during the earthquake and is now being remodelled as a more upmarket establishment. Other options include Newa Home, Hotel Northfield, Marsyangdi, Mandap, Manang, Avataar, Potala Guest House, Utse and Vaisali. For a taste of Tibet, try the Hotel Tibet in Lazimpat; nearby the Hotel Ambassador is being rebuilt. For greater luxury, lodge at the Hotel Malla on the edge of Thamel. En route to Swayambhunath is the traditional-style Hotel Vajra. The Hotel Shankar (a former Rana palace) and the palatial Yak and Yeti or Annapurna hotels suit more well-heeled guests. Around Boudhanath there are many hotels to suit all budgets. The heritage-style boutique hotel of Dwarika's is near the airport and restored Ram Mandir temple.

Eating out

For returning trekkers, Kathmandu and Pokhara are a paradise of over-indulgence. Choose your food very carefully before your trek – there is nothing worse than bumping along Nepal's 'main roads' with an upset stomach, except lurching along a 'side road' with an urgent need!! Even in the better restaurants, avoid salads and unpeeled fruit as a precaution. The following are a few of the popular eating places in Kathmandu (in no particular order; exclusion does not imply any criticism): Northfield Café, La Bella Café & Aqua Bar, The Ship, Green Organic Café, KC's, Pilgrims 24, Rum Doodle, Helena's, Yin Yang and Third Eye, Dechenling Garden, Kathmandu Guest House, Pumpernickel, Bamboo Club, New Orleans, Nargila's, Gaia, OR2K, Himalayan Java Café, La

Dolce Vita, Roadhouse Café, Delima Garden, Electric Pagoda, Utse, Fire and Ice, and The Factory. A reasonable meal will cost from Rs600–Rs1000 per person for a main dish, pizza, steak, curry and so on. Popular watering holes are Sam's, Tom & Jerry and various Irish Pubs!

Tourist office

This office is located in Bhrikuti Mandap, near Ratna Park bus station. National Park/Conservation Area permits and TIMS are issued here.

Pokhara – after the trek

Pokhara (900m) has boomed over the years into a sprawling but still pleasant town of a considerable size. It was once a sleepy village surrounded by rice fields and some very dense jungle. Lakeside is the main tourist area, where hotels, restaurants and shops are found. There are not many historic sites in Pokhara, but it does have an old bazaar street and the Pokhara Mountain Museum. High above the placid Phewa Lake is the Peace Pagoda. Tibetan refugee camps are located around the town and to the southeast is the narrow ravine of Devi's Falls. Of course it's easy just to eat, sleep and muck about in a boat on the lake after a hard trek. Sarangkot is a spectacular vantage point, to watch the sunrise or sunset on the Annapurna ranges, untainted, brooding and standing sentinel over the valley.

Accommodation

Pokhara has hotels and guest houses to suit all budgets. The expensive Fishtail Lodge is a good place for afternoon tea on the lawn. In Lakeside is the beautifully designed Heritage Hotel and Suites, along with many old favourites such as the cosy Peace Eye Guest House, Snowlands (once a thatched farmhouse), Hungry Eye, Rising Moon Guest House, Meera, Café in the Garden and many more.

Eating out

Pokhara Lakeside has places to satisfy every cuisine and taste of returning trekkers, tourists and idle, ageing hippies. There are some great new places, too many to name. Indian food lovers mention the long-established Punjabi Restaurant.

Tourist office
This office is located in the Damside area of Pokhara. Permits and TIMS are normally issued here.

Other places of interest
Those with more time often visit the following places after a trek.

Bandipur
Up in the hills just south of the road from Kathmandu to Pokhara is the small traditional hilltop village of Bandipur. With great mountain views, fresh air and many beautifully restored old buildings and temples, this historic village is fast becoming a popular getaway and stopover. (www.rural-heritage.com)

Riepe/Chowk Chisopani
Just to the north along the road to Besisahar is Riepe, near Chowk Chisapani, where another rural development offers fabulous views of the Annapurnas, Lamjung, Manaslu and Himalchuli. (www.annapurnahomestay.com)

Gorkha
Gorkha has a reasonable selection of hotels, so it's worth stopping overnight here to visit the famed Durbar Palace. Gorkha has rapidly expanded from a two-horse country bazaar into a sizeable town with hotels, guesthouses, bus syndicate wheeler-dealers and wily horse-traders.

Nuwakot
This ancient settlement sits almost pristinely on the ridge top, just 8km off the road to Langtang. Its ancient palace has been a fortified stronghold for centuries. Being in command of the important trading crossroads of the Trisuli Valley, it exacted tolls and duties on goods flowing between India and Tibet. See www.rural-heritage.com

Chitwan National Park
The most popular and easily accessed National park, Chitwan is located south of the Kathmandu–Pokhara road not far from Narayanghat. Rhinos, sloth bear, deer, a variety of birds and gharals are most frequently sighted. Elephants are used for some jungle safaris.

Using this guide on the trails
The following trekking route descriptions (and road routes) indicate approximate distances, timings and altitudes. Maps of the trekking routes sometimes show different figures, so it is has been necessary in places to give a 'guestimate' for altitudes. The trekking marches described mostly correlate to day-to-day itineraries, but not at every stage. The itineraries shown in the appendix summary section reflect the possible routes and durations. With time and energy, it's perfectly possible to combine the treks described. The suggested trek itinerary appendix also gives a rough grade of difficulty.

Much debate between trekkers centres on the accuracy of daily trekking times in guidebooks. This edition will no doubt raise the same issues. What is average for one trekker is desperately hard or astonishingly easy for another. The times shown are an attempt to give the average time for the walk, with extra time added to cover a few photo stops, pausing to tie up a bootlace, and for those quick visits into the vegetation. A trek in the Himalaya is supposed to be an enriching experience and a holiday. A trek is not, for most hikers, a competition to see who can climb to the Dhaulagiri Sanctuary faster than a pilgrim seeking to cleanse a serious misdemeanour. It's probable that independent trekkers without guides or porters will find our timings on the slow side – please adjust your expectations to accommodate our times.

We have not attempted to list all the lodges along all the trails! There is often little to choose between them – it is usually determined by where you happen to be by late afternoon and which place catches your attention.

New 'roads'
As a rule, the effect of a new road in Nepal is rather negative, with the creation of noise, pollution, dust clouds and chaos for pedestrians. Inevitably the destruction of the once-pristine environment is noticed quickly. Most of the 'new roads' are little more than farm tracks, meaning rough rides, dust or mud, delays due to avalanches, floods and bridge washouts. The journey time is never set in stone. Bear this in mind when planning your itinerary, anywhere.

Trekkers who visited Nepal some time ago lament the coming of roads, but from a Nepalese point of view this is progress. There is no more humping of ridiculously heavy loads along narrow, exposed, slippery trails or crossing precarious log bridges, not to mention the leeches. Generally local people are in favour of new access dirt roads, since they significantly reduce food prices.

As temporary visitors it's hard to disagree with local dwellers, who have to pay high prices for goods. The main downside of the new country roads is that some people who earn money from passing trekkers are going to lose their most valued asset – those passing trekkers. The trekker today has to take the treks as they are now. Nepal is there to change you, and not for you to change it. Experience so far suggests that very few hikers are put off by the quiet, almost traffic-free, jeep roads close to trails – just look at the Annapurnas, where the numbers of trekkers has increased.

You would hardly think there is any need to define a road in so many ways, but in Nepal nothing ever quite conforms to the norms.

Sealed road: A tarmac highway – but expect potholes and even broken-up sections.
Jeep track: Any side road used by jeeps and tractors.
Wide trail: A regular trail, often one that the mule caravans have used for centuries, which may end up being a dirt road.

Of course roads and trails will change – sometimes surprisingly fast, Please make allowance for these changes when evaluating this guide – *Dhanyabad*!

Spies on the roof of the world

Today GPS and satellites can give us an accurate altitude for any given point but 150 years ago there was another way. Water boils at a lower temperature at higher altitude and this may be noticed by trekkers. What is less commonly known is that the measurement of that boiling point can actually be used to determine the altitude with surprising accuracy.

When the British colonial administration in India felt threatened by the Russians and Chinese during the 'Great Game' in the 19th century, they sent spies into Tibet to discover the geography of that great blank on the map. These spies, known as the pandits, were Indians, who could easily travel in disguise as pilgrims, measuring miles with rosary beads and altitudes with thermometers.

The most famous pandit was Sarat Chandra Das, a Bengali and Tibetan scholar, whose exploits are recorded in his book A Journey to Lhasa and Central Tibet. He measured the boiling point of the water at Kambachen (Kanchenjunga region) as 187°F, calculating the height as 13,600ft (4145m). Today we have all manner of dubious listening devices, so little has changed!

Pre-trek checklist

Don't trek alone: hire a guide.
Don't set off without your national park, conservation area and restricted area permit(s).
Register your journey with your embassy (if trekking independently).
Have adequate insurance for yourself and your staff.
Carry a photocopy of your passport/visa details page.
Carry a first aid kit and medications.
Be forewarned about the dangers of altitude and act accordingly.
Treat porters properly.
Register with the checkposts.
Respect the culture, the environment and local sensibilities.
Dress appropriately. Watch your step!

Nyatapola temple, Bhaktapur

Enjoy your trek!

THE TREKKING ROUTES

Not all those who wander are lost.
Lord of the Rings, **J R R Tolkien**

Dhaulagiri Sanctuary Trek

Introduction
Dhaulagiri is the seventh highest mountain in the world and its name means dazzling mountain or white peak. Quite often it is the first of the giant Himalayan peaks that appears on the flight into Kathmandu from the west. Its massive south face dominates the skyline until Annapurna is in view later. Almost no one has been to the Dhaulagiri Sanctuary, so this is a pioneering trek route. The last stage of the trail to the south base camp is expected to be constructed in the monsoon season of 2018.

The Dhaulagiri region is a kaleidoscope of different cultures, colourful festivals, varied vegetation, astonishing scenery and, most of all, welcoming people. So far tourism has had hardly any impact on the local people. Village life continues much as it always has. Change is inevitable as new roads and mobile phone networks begin to intrude.

No trek in the Himalaya offers much flat walking and these valleys are no different. There are a few opportunities in the greater area of the Sanctuary to add your own amount of 'toil and trouble'. It's not necessary to cross any high pass, thus avoiding any potentially blocking obstacles like the Thorong La on the Annapurna Circuit or the Larkya La around Manaslu. There are high passes to the side of the main route, but they will only concern those setting out to tackle them as part of their plan.

Of course some days are hard, and bitterly cold conditions can be encountered higher up. Homestays are often basic and sometimes the food may take what seems like hours to come. However, as with any trek in Nepal, the joys of the journey far outweigh the hardships.

Planning

Unlike many treks that go to great altitudes, there are few obvious headaches on this short trek. Following the basic route into the Dhaulagiri Sanctuary allows a multitude of environments to be experienced while not going higher than 4100m. Side trips of varying degrees of strenuousness are mentioned in the appropriate sections. Parts of the trail require special care and attention; short stages of exposure are encountered.

The majority of trekkers will only suffer minor effects of altitude if planning enough time. Altitude problems are most likely to occur when climbing the last stage into the Sanctuary itself. Shorter days en route and an intermediate camp between Odar and South Base Camp should avoid most stubborn effects. In any case it's easy to retreat downwards if symptoms persist.

With only a few homestays, no lodges and no trail signs on overgrown paths, taking a guide is necessary at the moment. Currently having a porter/porters is also desirable for all but the strongest trekkers, since there are no facilities above Phedi. Camping and carrying all food is essential. Ideally it would be best to hire porters locally, but this is becoming quite difficult as more and more younger people head for the cities. A good local trekking outfit would be in a better position to help, but they too are rare. Finding porters in Kathmandu can be daunting, so ask at one of the many trekking agencies; see appendix 5.

In March we encountered a large ice sheet near Odar Camp that will stop all those without an ice axe, rope and mountaineering gear. This ice sheet runs down steeply from the cliffs for 200m straight into the river. It is around 25–30m across. We are informed that it does not exist after the monsoon, but being prepared is vital just in case it does! See more in the trekking description later.

Regarding the weather, be sure to avoid the higher areas in early spring unless you relish icy conditions. March and April are popular for those enjoying the rhododendron and orchid show. However, it can be especially hot in the lower reaches in April.

Avoid the monsoon – it's horribly cloudy, often raining and the leeches are voracious. Just after the monsoon and until mid-October, the higher areas suffer from lingering snow. In fact recently the weather patterns have been much more unreliable. Be prepared for changeable weather. The best time for a trek here for the views is in November and the first weeks of December. The days are a dream once the sun is up and it can be seriously hot at midday. Skies can be clear all day but the nights will be quite chilly to freezing higher up. Wind tends to be less of an issue during the autumn season, but spring can experience more breeze.

It is necessary to take a sleeping bag; homestay blankets are not always clean and might be unavailable, bed bugs are determined critters, and if bad weather persists for days, it gets very cold. As with all treks in the big mountains, it pays to have some of those goodies like chocolate that anyone craves on a long trek.

Itineraries and routes
Getting from Kathmandu to Pokhara, the options are between flying, taking a private vehicle or a bus (good or bad). The road to Beni is currently quite broken in places. A jeep road climbs up to the picturesque village of Jhi, with views of Dhaulagiri already on hand to inspire. The normal itinerary would allow time to travel out to the country town of Beni and onwards up the jeep track to Jhi in one day. However, things don't always go to plan, so it would be wise to allow a free day or two in Pokhara at the end of the trek in case this day becomes a day and a half.

The basic trek follows the Raghuganga Khola valley in and out for most of the way. Heading north, the route passes through Pakhapani, Kotgaon and Ulleri to Rayakhor. Climbing onwards, the path passes through Mulpani to Ghyasikharka, below Dhar and on to Chhari, the last settlement. Cloud rainforest and dense jungle dominate the way up to Phedi. After this a new trail climbs around the cliffs on the east through to Odar Camp and into the defile that guards the Sanctuary. The last haul into this treasury of the gods is spectacular, to within a yak's whisker of the unbelievably soaring south face of Dhaulagiri.

Returning from Phedi, an alternative trail on the east side of the valley after Ghyasikharka is on offer. This trail and dirt road lead through Chimkhola to Dagnam and eventually back to Beni by jeep.

The absolute minimum for this trek as far as Phedi, one of the best viewpoints, from Kathmandu and back is 10 days, but this is pushing luck to the limit. For the complete trek from Kathmandu, plan on at least 12–14 days for a better experience.

A comprehensive summary of routes and itinerary options for the Dhaulagiri Sanctuary/South Base Camp Trek is given in the appendix. The trek normally starts from the market town of Beni.

Dhaulagiri Sanctuary Trek Summary	
Start	**Beni** (830m)
Finish	**Beni** (830m)
Distance	approx. 60–70km (38–44 miles)
Time	12–14 days
Maximum altitude	**Sanctuary** (4100m/13,450ft)
Trekking style	Homestay and camping
Transport	Bus, jeep and plane

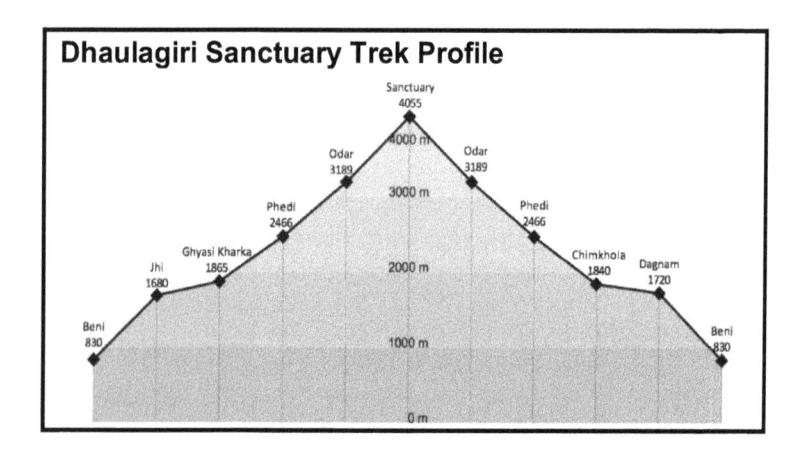

Dhaulagiri Sanctuary Trek Profile

Sanctuary 4055
Odar 3189
Odar 3189
Phedi 2466
Phedi 2466
Ghyasi Kharka 1865
Jhi 1680
Chimkhola 1840
Dagnam 1720
Beni 830
Beni 830

Dhaulagiri

Dhaulagiri is the world's seventh-highest mountain (8167m/26,795ft). In Sanskrit its name means 'white mountain'. Admired by thousands of trekkers from the Kali Gandaki and Poon Hill, Dhaulagiri resisted the attempts of mountaineers for much longer than comparable peaks. In 1950, Herzog's French expedition had initially hoped to summit it, but after lengthy reconnaissance decided it was too dangerous, turning their attention to Annapurna I instead. Six attempts on Dhaulagiri via the west ridge followed, but it was not until 1960 that a Swiss expedition finally won through – albeit in controversial style. They used a light aircraft to ferry food, equipment and even climbers to the northeast col at around 5700m (18,700ft). The Pilatus Porter, piloted by daredevils including Emil Wick, eventually crashed on the mountain without loss of life. Austrian mountaineer Kurt Diemberger, a 'foreigner' within the Swiss expedition, reached the summit on 13 May, in company with Peter Diener, Ernst Forrer, Albin Schelbert and the Sherpas Nyima Dorji and Nawang Dorji. Two other members (Michel Vaucher and Hugo Weber) also reached the top 10 days later. Attempts since then have tried different routes, but many have perished on the killer white mountain, particularly in avalanches from the notorious Dhaulagiri Icefall.

Kathmandu – Pokhara (30mins or 6–8hrs)
Kathmandu – Mugling – Pokhara

For a relaxed and more enjoyable trip, plan on going no further than Pokhara the first day, unless time is at a premium. Those with less time and more money might want to fly between Kathmandu and Pokhara and continue on to Beni by private jeep. Direct minibuses run from Kathmandu to Beni, taking at least 10hrs.

Currently the best bus is the Greenline service, with a tasty buffet in **Riverside Springs** near **Mugling** en route included. Other tourist buses are also an option, such as Swiss Bus.

An overnight local bus service operates direct from Kathmandu to Beni (cost Rs750–900). However, it's not recommended for trekkers even if the crew like the option!

Pokhara of course is a place not to be missed. The amazingly close, spectacular Annapurna peaks dominate the northern skyline. Pokhara is busting with hotels, guesthouses and good restaurants. It's so pleasant that some might never get away into the trekking hills!

Pokhara – Jhi (3–4 + 1½–2hrs)
Pokhara – Beni – Kushma – Jhi

Public buses and some jeeps leave for Beni from the Ganesh Tol, Baglung bus park in the city area. Buses (cost Rs210+) are slower and take almost 4hrs; a jeep (Rs3500–4000) takes 3hrs. It's 81 'fun-filled' kilometres to Beni from Pokhara.

The not-always-good road leaves Pokhara going west and up along the Naudanda ridge, with its great views of the Annapurna range. Then it snakes down from **Khare** (Kande) via **Lumle** to **Naya Phul** and along the Modi Khola valley. The stage from Naya Phul to **Kushma** is better but has also deteriorated in places. After Kushma the road joins the famous Kali Gandaki valley and continues on, mostly contouring northwest to **Beni** (830m).

Apart from the dusty bus park and the busy bazaar, there is not much to see in Beni. Those with more time could hike up to the former Malla fort above the town on the east side of the Kali Gandaki. A rough jeep road also leads up to this fort, soon to be converted into a hotel. Beni was a strategic centre on the former salt trade route between India and Tibet along the Kali Gandaki.

The town has a few acceptable hotels if time or lack of an onward jeep is an issue. By the noisy bus park are the Hotel Muktinath, Mustang Lete Hotel, Old Lete Mustang Hotel and one other. The Yak Hotel, a block back from the road, is said to be the best place in town. Anything better is likely to be full of NGOs.

It might be better to arrange a private jeep here to save time and hassle. We booked with Subba Magar: tel 9867608421. From Beni, jeeps head from near a big tree on the south area of the main bazaar. From here it's immediately uphill on a rough and bumpy dirt track classified as a road. Quite soon there are views of Beni below and the Kali Gandaki heading southeast. The road keeps to the east side of the main ridge. There are a few settlements, such as **Arate** and **Patiekhet** en route, and any excuse for a stop for a photo is welcomed. There are views east of the Nilgiri peaks, Tilicho, Annapurna I, Fang and Annapurna South. Dhaulagiri also takes a bow later en route.

The substantial village of **Jhi** (1680m) is a picturesque place, with traditional Magar houses painted in red/terracotta and white. Most are stone and rectangular in shape with slate roofing: the original style. As more jeeps ply the dirt road from Beni, expect concrete, tin and gaudy colours to take over.

At the moment Jhi has a few homestay options, although in reality these are just people's houses rearranged for the 'odd' guest. There are a couple of temples nearby; one is at Todke.

Jhi Magar village

Side trip: Todke viewpoint (4–5hrs)

Directly above the village to the west is Todke hill. If a jeep is available, it takes around 30mins one way up the dirt road to the viewpoint. On a clear day the western Annapurna peaks and Dhaulagiri are stunning. If you have lots of time, the trek up takes about 2½hrs; the trail begins at the north end of the village near a small shrine. A local guide is necessary. Also on the ridge is a small temple near the Ncell telecoms tower.

Stage 1: Jhi to Rayakhor

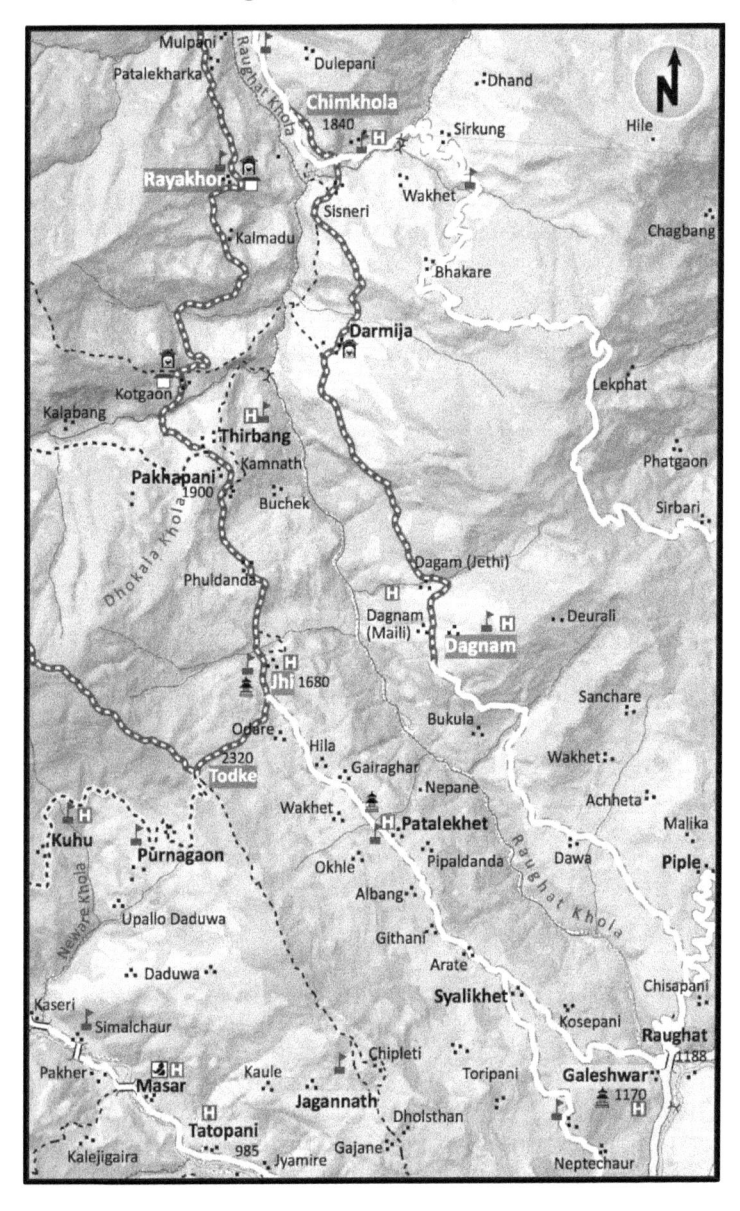

The Magar people

Unlike the Sherpas, Tamangs and Gurungs, the Magar people are one of the less well-known clans in Nepal. Many loosely adhere to Hindu traditions but a few adhere to Buddhist practices. Most, though, are more inclined to animism and the worship of nature, the elements and their ancestors than either of the two main faiths. Magars are not confined to this valley but are found across the Myagdi district as well as being scattered across the whole of Nepal. Some people with Tibetan ancestry also call themselves Magar, particularly across Dolpo and West Nepal. The Magars and the Chantyals, who are also common in the region, perform animal sacrifices. They worship deities with names such as Kuldebata, Barah, Sime Bhume and Mandali.

Jhi – Rayakhor (5–6hrs)
Jhi – Pakhapani – Ulleri – Rayakhor

It's the first day of trekking and it's a relief to be away from the lovely buses and jolly jeeps. Well, isn't it? The day is varied, relatively gentle, with stacks of interest; expect farms, hill terraces, woodlands and dramatic cliff views. Getting as far as Ghyasikharka is a tall order, so plan on making it to Rayakhor. In fact there is a stunning panoramic view of Dhaulagiri from Rayakhor, perhaps the best on the whole trek.

The dirt road continues out of Jhi; at a corner take a shortcut across the old trail suspension bridge. A steady climb follows along the road close to **Phuldanda** for around 40mins. Leaving the dirt road, the route heads off up to the right at a corner near a shrine. Climbing on the steepening path, there are two more shrines devoted to Shiva. One is a rounded structure. Both have tridents on top and one has a vague rock-like image of Nandi Bull inside. There is another temple higher up and then the path re-joins the road and the bus stop before **Pakhapani** (1900m). The Annapurna peaks poke out briefly near here to the east.

From the white gleaming school of Pakhapani the trail descends on a grassy path and some stone steps. It's quite a steep descent past a couple of houses. Just after a small bridge and shrine is the main bridge over the Ghopte

Khola. A steep climb, often on steps, ensues to Kotgaon (1900m). The name suggests this place once had a fort (Kot) but evidence today is sparse. It's a rabbit warren of narrow alleys, closely packed traditional terracotta and white houses in stone and slate. We found lunch of dal bhat at a local house, but beware the costs here and ask first. Dal bhat was an amazingly costly Rs500 each for us and the crew!

Hardly before leaving Kotgaon the path again ascends to the village school. An easy workout for the children in the morning, but not perhaps for first-day fresh-smelling trekkers! After the school the trail drops easily into a side tributary to a bridge and waterfall. Cliffs dominate the area as well as a plethora of orchids and rhododendrons. A steady uphill follows through thinning woodland to a porters' rest stop with views back to Jhi. Extensive terracing is evident to the south.

The trail, which is good here, climbs to another porter rest area with views east down to Darmija village. Ahead is a dramatic cliff face. The route climbs beside outcrops before descending from the crest to **Ulleri** and a suspension bridge. There are views across to Chimkhola now and the rushing torrent of the Raghuganga Khola.

Like its namesake on the Ghorepani trek in the nearby Annapurnas, this Ulleri is also associated with steps. However, this next lot are not so demanding and lead up to the settlement of **Rayakhor** (2075m). It's a fabulous location perched on top of a dramatic cliff, which is only seen later from the eastern trail. There are no real homestays, just a willing local or two with a spare room. Our 'homestay' was the local alehouse and bridges the path. A room cost Rs200 and dal bhat Rs150.

Stage 2: Rayakhor to Phedi

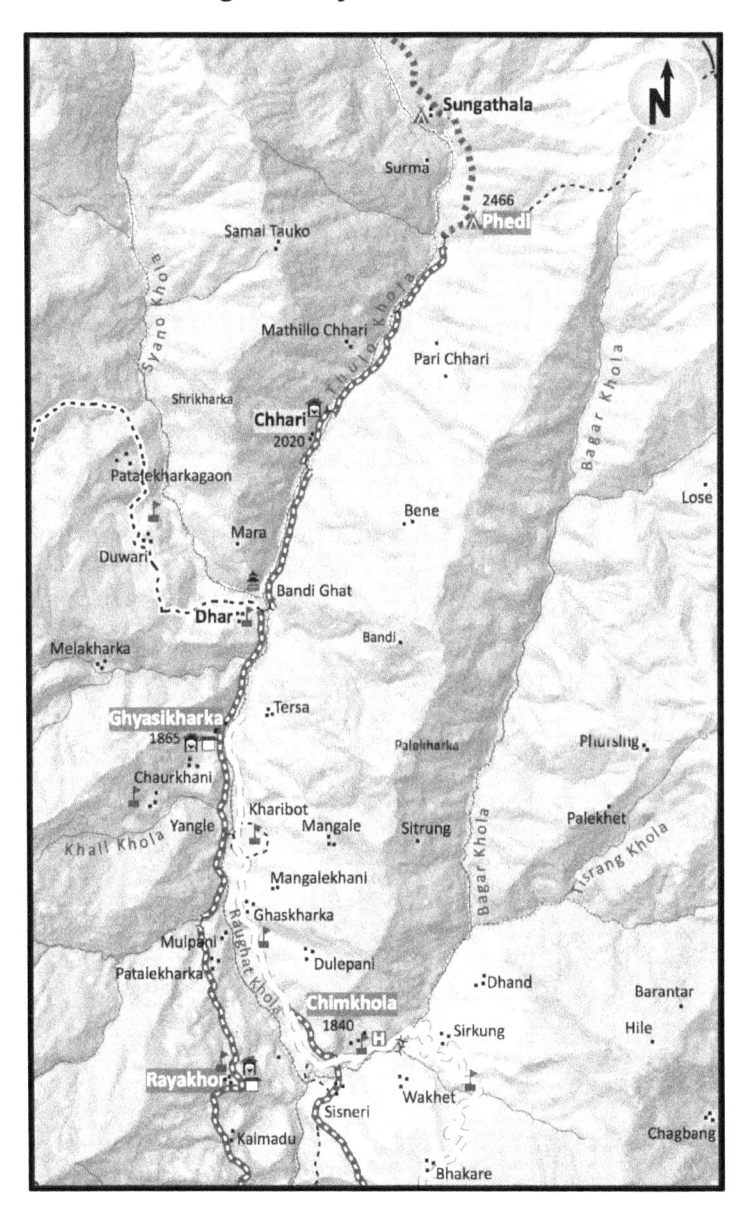

Rayakhor – Chhari (5–6hrs)
Rayakhor – Ghyasikharka – Chhari

This is another superb day, especially if the dawn is clear and bright. The view north to Jirbang, Manapati and Dhaulagiri is stunning at sunrise and for the whole morning's walk. The villages are picture-postcard and the trail a delight through varied countryside. Camping begins at the one-house settlement of Chhari, the last human habitation on the route to Base Camp.

From Rayakhor the trail goes gently down through thinning woods with spindly trees to a landslide zone.

Be careful where the trail, composed of mica schist, is slippery, especially if it's been raining. There are some steps and a small walled meadow as the route crosses the old (and new) landslide zones. The views of Dhaulagiri continue to be stupendous. A brief ascent follows on the 'exciting' – that means a little exposed – path. Soon it's down again through isolated farms and striking rhododendron trees.

Below Rayakhor

A more concentrated descent leads through the farms, collectively called **Mulpani** (est 1950m). This place is also called Patelkharka on another map. En route ahead is a view of **Sarbang Dhuri** peak and the **Ruwachaur Himal** ridge.

The trail crosses a tributary on a suspension bridge and continues down to a porter resting spot just above the main Raghuganga River. Heading along above the main river, the route crosses another good suspension bridge before climbing up through the houses o**f Yanglekhan**. Again climbing a little, the path crosses the Khali Khola on another suspension bridge. Be careful in the fields next; the trail disappears briefly before climbing around a bluff. Ahead it ascends gently, with the first bamboos on show. After a drier zone, the trail is rockier underfoot but soon the sports field of **Ghyasikharka** (1865m) is reached. It's around 3hrs from Rayakhor to here. The village is lower than Jhi; oh no, all that up and down for no overall altitude gain!

You may be able to find someone to cook dal bhat in one of the houses in the main village cluster. Inevitably more and better homestay/lodge places will develop, but for now it's better to camp if overnighting here. Of course for some, homestay is what they seek in order to have a more 'authentic' experience and they won't be disappointed here. Others might crave more comforts; better stick to the Annapurna Circuit! Old people like us might need to bring thermarests to disguise the hard beds. There's no satisfying some!

High above the village are some terraced fields clinging to the north face of a massive outcrop near the upper inhabited part of the village called Chaurkhani.

From the main part of the village, the trail heads along to a poor bridge that crosses to the school, one of the better houses for homestay and the route to Chimkhola. Keep to the west bank and continue along the main river to the hydro plant. The route climbs gently to a suspension bridge across the Raghuganga Khola just below the unseen settlement of **Dhar**.

This settlement lies just up around the corner on a good wide trail that climbs from the suspension bridge, still on the west side. This trail also leads to the **Sapta Rishi shrine** far beyond the next, and last, village of **Duwari**.

> **Sapta Rishi shrine**
> Lying high above the valley of the Syano and Lamph Kholas is the shrine of Sapta Rishi. According to legends, seven (sapta) rishis or sadhus spent years in retreat here in deep meditation. It is said that so deep was their meditation that they created the rice plant for the people of the land. Indeed they are credited with giving rice to the world. And so it came to pass that trekkers can eat piles of rice (bhat) with dal across Nepal due to these pious sadhus. The main festival at Sapta Rishi is Janai Purnima, celebrated in August, and similar to the same festival at Gosainkund Lake on the Langtang/Helambu trek. Some maps show a pass from the shrine over the Jirbang ridge to the Dhaulagiri Base Camp area but it's not a viable option for trekkers.

Side trip: Bandi Ghat shrines

Also by the Raghuganga suspension bridge is a small path leading to the two shrines of **Bandi Ghat**. The path starts below the suspension bridge, heading northwards and winding around small fields in the trees and boulders for 5–10mins on the level – wow! A good but narrow log bridge crosses the Syano Khola to reach the twin shrines.

> **Warning:**
> Be very respectful at the Bandi Ghat shrines and if the local people are offended by your visit do not venture too close to the shrines. This site is used for cremation funeral pyres and people believe that outsiders may disturb the ancestors and bring bad luck. There is not much to see that cannot be viewed from across the river on the trail up to Chhari, especially with a good camera or binoculars.

When leaving the shrines, a path on this west side of the Raghuganga Khola, used by shepherds, follows the bank to a scary-looking bridge across the main river. If this option looks too scary, return to the long suspension bridge and cross the Raghuganga Khola there.

Bandi Ghat shrines

The first structure is a square, four-tiered, pagoda-style Shiva temple. A couple of bells hang around the outside with some butter lamps. The interior chamber probably houses a lingam-shaped object. The second structure, probably a Parvati (Shiva's wife) shrine, is very unusual in that it is three-sided. It has three tiers. Between the two shrines are three metal Nandi bull images representing the 'vehicle' of Shiva. If you are allowed to visit, it takes about 30mlns for a side trip here.

Once across the river, the trail climbs steeply to a more level area with the two shrines still in view below.

The trail ascends further, with some short but steeper sections through a grassy clearing or two. The whole valley is becoming narrow, hemmed in by increasingly steeper-sided slopes and mysterious forest. The path is quite wet as it makes for an abandoned shed set in some fields.

Continuing along through the wild and dank forest, the path comes to a suspension bridge back across the Raghuganga Khola to the one-house settlement of **Chhari** (2020m).

Camp in Chhari

The welcoming family of Bhakti Prasad Chantyal at Chhari have little to offer in the way of accommodation, unless desperate, but the crew enjoyed the good home-grown organic food.

The paddock is a bit muddy after rain, but the people here are very industrious. Their dog has an equal amount of energy, usually at night, so camp further away down the fields near the abandoned house to avoid a noisy interlude. There's not much to do in Chhari, although the cicadas might provide a rousing chorus at times.

Chhari – Phedi (4–5hrs)
Chhari – No-bridge stream – Phedi

From here onwards the route traverses dense, eerie jungle, climbing into wild pristine, soggy cloud forest. Be sure to carry warm clothing for the cold afternoon. Before Phedi imposing cliffs and hillsides restrict the views. Phedi is set high above the valley.

After Chhari the route heads gently up, passing a water mill and continuing along an irrigation channel before crossing it to the right. A few stepping stones and then a flimsy-looking bridge carry all across to the east bank of the Raghuganga.

Immediately the path enters a wonderland of cloud forest with some mossy glades along the riverbank to entice. It's sometimes confusing, because the little-used trail is often carpeted with dead leaves. Further along, look for a point on the opposite bank where a side stream joins the main river. Around here the trail turns uphill to the right, below a big tree.

There are quite a few big trees around here, some bigger than others! Route-finding is hard, but root-finding is easy! It is hard to believe this was once a shortcut trading route from Jhi to Tibet.

The trail climbs on a wet path into more dense forest before 'contouring' with some ups and downs. At a side stream, head upwards around a big rock to the right instead of trying to negotiate the streambed and a wooden ladder structure. Then it is steeply up around a cliff bluff and then even more steeply into a side ravine. The path has been well engineered here, many moons ago. The narrow, exposed stage is short but quite high above the river. Another stream is easily crossed and then it's up again to a vague junction. Descend here. The upper trail at the junction is steep and has a view 2mins up, but it's not a good choice.

The route continues on a narrow trail in dense forest, still going up to another vague junction. This time the upper trail is better, heading up and around to a small open kharka where nettles have taken charge. Let's call it **Nettles Kharka**. Nettle soup (sisnu) is a very nutritious and a popular addition to the local diet, but don't eat too much unless you have constipation! This spot is about 1hr 45mins from Chhari.

Slipping steeply down now on a wet path, the trail crosses a bridgeless side stream to reach an open area. This makes a great lunch spot and could also be a good camping place with a sunny aspect (if it's not raining!). It is marked on the Dhaulagiri Sanctuary map as a wooden bridge although there is no bridge here. We can call it **No-bridge stream** (2200m) for now, about 2hrs from Chhari.

Tearing oneself away from the idyllic meadow, the trail climbs steeply (they always do after a big dollop of rice and potatoes). It's up and up to a side stream for 30mins and another 5mins more after that to the temporary 'topside'. Now follows the inevitable descent, but not so far, to a log bridge. The nearby stepping-stones are a lot healthier to use. Soon enough a steep ascent starts, up to a clearing (a possible camping place if required, although not so flat). This place should be called Phedi (1hr from the No-bridge stream lunch spot) as it's at the bottom of a big hill like most Phedis in Nepal.

However an anomaly occurs here, the objective of the day, Phedi Camp, is further up a big hill. This lower place must be **Phedi Phedi**!

The route gets confusing here. There was a framework shelter here, over to the right where a vague path exists in the dip. Head up and shortly to the right is a deep canyon filled with a rushing stream and waterfalls. One path is off left after about 5mins. We went too high up here to a half diamond-triangular rock and turned sharp left on a vague path.

On our descent, we came into the dip lower down on yet another vague path. It's a bit of trial and error, but either route will suffice. If you get lost, ask a policeman!

Once out into a more open forest area, the trail zigzags up to another clearing and in a further 10mins open ground is reached. Zigzagging up steeply across the grassy slope, the way soon arrives at a large open area of sloping ground – the real **Phedi** (2466m)! There are only about three vaguely flat places to camp at the moment and the water source is to the south, towards the rushing stream seen on the way up. (Note that one map suggests there is no water here, but that is not true as far as we know, unless it applies after exceptionally dry weather). Currently there is no porter or cooking shelter at Phedi, although plans for some construction do exist. Throwing a tarpaulin over the odd bamboo frameworks must suffice for now.

We were unable to locate the trail to Lete here, although it definitely exists.

If lady luck smiles on you, there is a fantastic view of Dhaulagiri from here at sunset and sunrise. Until the trail was cut higher up, this place gave the only really good view of the peak, which has been elusive for the last day or so. It's amazing how many of these deeply forested valleys hide the mountains from view, even when almost below their ramparts.

Of course it would be perfectly possible to plan a shorter trek just to Phedi taking 7–8 days from Pokhara.

Stage 3: Phedi to South Base Camp

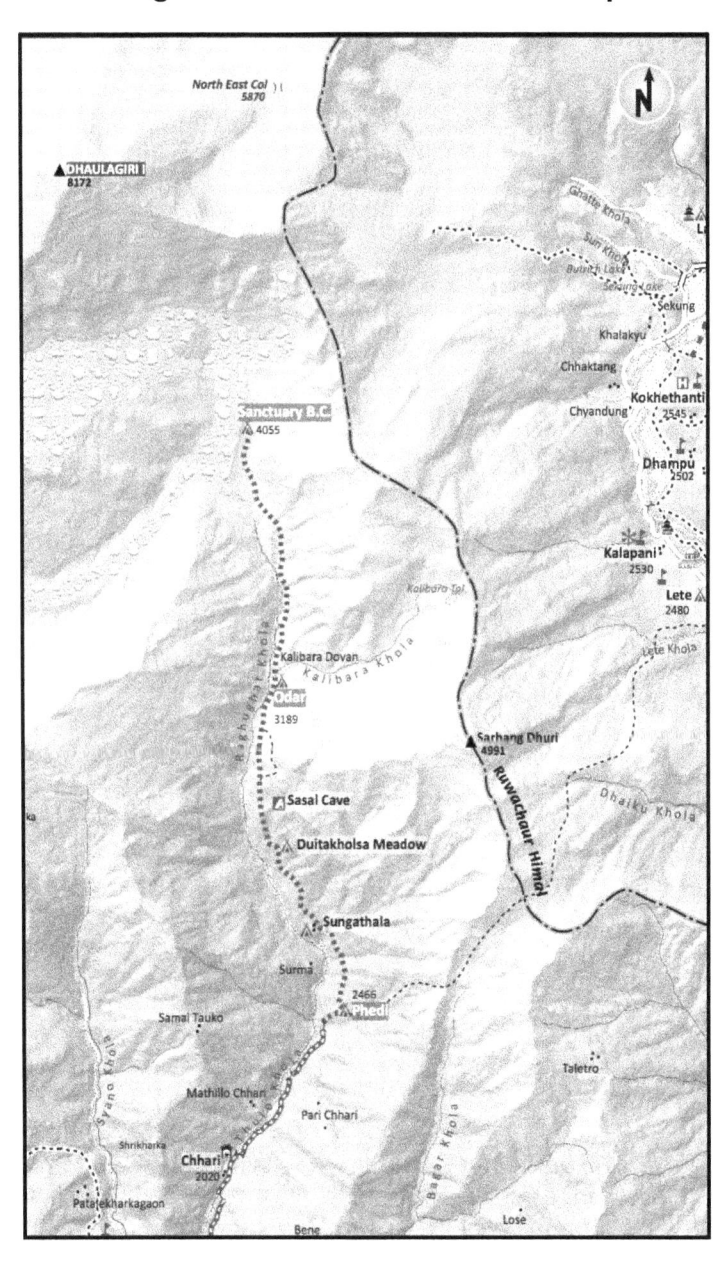

Phedi – Odar Camp (4–5hrs)
Phedi – Duitakholsa meadow – Odar Camp

This is normally one of the harder days on the trek, not because of the particularly difficult terrain, but because this is the first critical day in which altitude plays a part. Take it slowly, as there is no rush to get to Odar Camp. Again carry warm clothing for the cold afternoon. Hopefully at Phedi a glorious sunrise awaits at dawn. The view is sensational and it's worth coming only this far for those with limited time.

From Phedi the path heads around the hillside quite gently at the start. A couple of fallen trees blocked our path, requiring some extra effort. A slippery stage down is encountered before a stream and then the tangled roots and encroaching bamboos slow things a tad. Eventually the narrow path drops closer to the river to the more substantial side stream of the **Sungathala Khola** and **waterfall**.

A dodgy bridge (about 1hr 10mins from Phedi) here is best avoided; the stepping stones in the river are much more accommodating. Once across, there is a bit of a scramble up to regain the trail. There now follows a brutal zigzagging ascent. Don't think about the return descent for now! This challenging pull uphill lasts for around 35–40mins. After a possibly dry stream the trail emerges on to the open pastures of **Sungathala** (est 2550m) about 2hrs from Phedi. Sungathala is called Sungurthala by the locals; it means place of wild pigs/boars. We only encountered two lonely sheep. There is said to be water somewhere around here, so camping might be an option. Ask the sheep!

Finding the trail out is again an issue, but look for the blue painted signs BL13 and a 0 sign on a rock over to the northwest side of the clearing. Don't follow these blue markings as we did for a while; they are for a future hydro scheme – maybe! The correct path passes a large rectangular rock on the left adjacent to the route shortly after leaving the clearing. The trail now crosses a plateau area in less dense woodland. About 30mins from Sungathala is another much smaller open meadow with two streams.

This is **Duitakholsa Meadow** (2770m). Its name means two streams. It's a great lunch spot on the way up and a super washing and camping place on the way down. Nature feels very close in this idyllic, peaceful place. If you only get lost briefly, it's about 3hrs from Phedi. Despite the enchanting forest canopy, there is even a view of Dhaulagiri from the trail here just to the south of the clearing.

About 20mins up from Duitakholsa is a large riverbed to cross on a rocky path. It was dry in March. The trail gets increasingly steeper now in the forest. At a junction go left. The trail to the right leads to a cave overhang, which is a good place to shelter if it's raining heavily.

This place is called **Sasal Cave**. The stream nearby is the same as the one crossed earlier. It is apparently dry for much of the time. Sometimes when it's not dry an amazing shower (said to number a hundred) of dripping mini waterfalls are on display.

Sasal Cave overhang

The wild forest was once, and still may be, the home of black bears and other timid creatures; perhaps leopards or a bigger cat that one would not like to encounter during a nocturnal excursion. The steep trail continues up, seemingly forever, for 45mins or more to a **small clearing** with a view of the landslide. Ahead is the cliff called **Sahashra Veer**. It is here that the new route keeps below the cliffs. The Beni Committee/HMH research expedition had to negotiate the cliffs! The new trail is an amazingly well engineered.

From the small clearing the route goes left and down briefly before contouring around the various bluffs of the cliffs. Across the valley is a towering waterfall. Hugging the river, the trail continues into a deep canyon, contouring around where sun is a luxury. The new path is quite wide in places, enough for a tent or two. There is a stream along here below the cliffs, but it's a slow trickle.

About 30mins from the clearing is the new **rock staircase** that negotiates the main cliff. It must have been very challenging for the team, mainly from Chimkhola, to construct this trail.

This rock stairway to heaven surmounts the cliff just above the Raghuganga river, passing a couple of rough flattish areas that might serve as campsites. After the main cliff, along the trail is a very low cave called **Odar Camp** (3189m). There is not much room; maybe two tents at the moment. Camping areas are expected to be made here or just a bit higher up in the bamboo thickets. Expect a cold night here.

Less than 10mins beyond Odar cave we encountered a massive sheet of ice that dropped directly into the Raghuganga Khola. This was a big surprise at only 3200m in spring. Ours was not a mountaineering expedition and this effectively stopped us in our tracks, as we were travelling light without an ice axe, although we did have a rope.

The ice sheet above Odar

What to do about this Ice sheet?
We were informed that this ice sheet is not normally in place after the monsoon and through the main autumn trekking season. It seems to appear after the winter, through the spring until mid-May. This means groups heading here in spring must carry ice axes, ropes and harnesses in order to cross this big obstacle. In autumn it should not be an issue, but there is a chance that this ice sheet comes from very high up, above the cliffs, and so might cause problems even then. Being fully prepared is the only viable course of action. The Beni committee might seek to build a couple of bridges here to get around it. One totally unsafe log structure can be seen to exist beyond the ice slide. Incidentally we did see some paw-prints in the vicinity. Perhaps this region is home to snow leopards.

Odar Camp – South Base Camp (3–5hrs)
Odar Camp – Kalibara Khola – South Base Camp

The following notes have been derived from our own observations, the Beni Committee/HMH team and Durba Paija (and his photographs taken above Odar). At the moment the trail does not exist in a form that porters can use. It's rough boulder-scrambling with some small cliffs and exposed stages. The Beni Committee is planning to construct the trail in the monsoon of 2018. Before setting out, do check whether this trail has been completed.

With another 800m of height gain from Odar the effects of altitude will be significant, so be aware of this on the hard climb. It might be necessary to make an intermediate camp before base camp. Some of the terrain is difficult, particularly where streams have to be crossed and boulders negotiated. That said, it's a day of high anticipation and excitement as the great mountain yields its secrets. Seen from such a close vantage point, the South Face of Dhaulagiri is stupendous. It has a completely different shape from so close yet so far below the summit.

In fact the summit is barely visible from Base Camp.

View towards Kalibarah Khola from the ice sheet

Assuming the ice sheet is overcome, soon after leaving Odar Camp is the side stream of the **Kalibarah Khola** (also spelt Kalibara). The name implies a dark secret and it's a sure bet that few humans have climbed to its upper reaches, where lies a lake named Kalibara Tsho. Getting to the lake could be a new side trip once the sanctuary trail is opened.

As if by magic, the toil gives way to euphoria as the high altitude meadows are attained, just below the glaciers that drape the colossal soaring face of Dhaulagiri and the long ridge around to Jirbang. **Dhaulagiri South Base Camp** (4055m) has a breathtaking view, say no more. Remember to keep up your fluid intake – that's more night calls, then! If it's full moon, that could be a delight to anticipate.

Currently it is expected that the **Dhaulagiri South Base Camp** as marked on the map will be the first place to be made ready. It does however have a slight risk of avalanche, according to the local people. Certainly avalanches do tumble from the south face.

Another camp area is likely to be made to the west, across the Raghuganga Khola. This **West Camp** (4100m) has a large area suitable for future development and gives access to various optional walks.

**Glacial source of the Raghuganga Khola
(photo: Durba Paija)**

Attempts on the South Face of Dhaulagiri

It's pretty astonishing that anyone could climb the south face of Dhaulagiri, but it was achieved on 15 October 1981.

Base camp was set at 3924m. After two weeks of reconnaissance, a Yugoslav team comprising Stane Belak Srauf, Cene Bercic and Emil Tratnik climbed from the right (east) side of the South Face for five days. From here they joined the Southeast Ridge at around 7185m; it took another four days to reach 7950m at the junction of the Southeast and Northeast Ridges. The last stage followed the original 1960 Swiss/Austrian route to the summit.

A Polish team led by Eugeniusz Chrobak in 1986 chose a route on the South Face, from the west side of the central buttresses. They climbed a 1200m rock wall on the prominent buttress left of the central face. The conditions proved extremely challenging, with poor rock, near vertical ice and all requiring 3200m of fixed rope. Maciej Berbeka and Mikolaj Czyzewski set Camp V on 30 October. High winds wrecked their tent and, despite making it higher, the climb was abandoned due to deteriorating weather.

Slovenian Tomaž Humar made another attempt of note in autumn 1999. Although he acclimatised on the north side, he made an attempt from South Base Camp, having flown there by helicopter. On 25 October he began his ascent on the South Face, with supplies for ten days. His planned route was to followed a direct line on the south face, but on his seventh day, Humar glimpsed the massive horizontal rock band above him. He realised that it would take two or three days to overcome this ferocious barrier. Taking various routes to avoid the great gully and the rock band, he then traversed about 1000m to the right to the southeast ridge. He eventually made it to 8000m on 02 November before abandoning his solo attempt.

Approaching the source of the Raghuganga and Dhaulagiri Sanctuary (photo: Durba Paija)

South Base Camp optional trips

Having made such an effort to get this far, most will want to linger in the Base Camp area for a day or so. It's also wise to plan an extra day into the trek in case an intermediate camp between Odar and South Base Camp is needed due to altitude issues.

North of Base Camp

One option is to climb along the moraine as far as possible (and as safe as is wise) northwards from Dhaulagiri South Base Camp. This route climbs higher, with the glacier to the left (west). We have no idea how far it is safe to go up here. Be aware of the avalanche risk in this general area.

West Camp viewpoints

Apparently there is a hill to the southwest of the West Camp flats, which offers a panoramic view from one of the highest possible spots. Astonishing views of the south wall of Dhaulagiri and westwards to the peaks Manapati and Jirbang are said to be on offer. We have no information about this option.

**Jirbang and Manapati from the Sanctuary
(photo: Durba Paija)**

Another option appears to be to walk westwards towards the peaks of Manapati and Jirbang (Jhirbang). The picture above suggests it's possible to hike some way towards the peaks. Once across the stream, there looks to be a route along the south moraine of the glacier for quite a long distance.

Kalibarah Tsho Lake

Herders and some pilgrims have been to the lake in the past but we have no information about the route or whether any trail exists. A future route might be possible over the ridge above the lake into the Kali Gandaki valley, but for now it's not on any agenda.

South Base Camp – Duitakholsa (5–6hrs)
South Base Camp – Odar – Duitakholsa

For those heading down after sunrise, this makes a good choice of routing. The camp in the forest at Duitakholsa (Two-streams) meadow is a delightful place. It should be possible to retreat this far once the new trail is built from Base Camp to Odar.

The trail from Odar descends around the new trail cliff path and after the rock staircase contours generally down around a few bluffs, some on regular footing, some on steps. After the **landslide view/small clearing** about 45mins down, it's a steep descent, so take particular care if it's wet. About 30mins down look for a small path off to the left to visit **Sasal Cave** for a late lunch or just as a side trip. It's less than 5 mins off the main trail.

From the junction it's only 30mins more to **Duitakholsa meadow**.

Duitakholsa – Chhari (6–7hrs)
Duitakholsa – Phedi – Chhari

This might seem to be a long slog down, but there are few places to camp. If you missed the view of Dhaulagiri from Phedi on the way up, it's worth stopping there. There is also the option of camping at No-Bridge stream meadow if Chhari proves too far.

The route begins easily across the generally flat plateau to the large open meadow at **Sungathala**, taking around 30mins. Now follows a very steep descent into the Sungathala Khola, with its waterfall eastwards to distract. Be very careful on this steep descent! Once across the stream below the dodgy bridge, it's back into the forest. Mostly it is fine, down and around the hillside, with a few ascents through bamboo. There is a short steep ascent before **Phedi** (2466m), about 2hrs or more from Duitakholsa.

From Phedi a rough and little-used woodcutters' trail crosses the **Ruwachaur Himal ridge** to Lete. There are plans to develop this very ancient trade route and summer herding trail. The herders graze both sheep and cows around a meadow called **Pairo Kharka**. See the Dhaulagiri Sanctuary Plus Trek for details.

From Phedi the path drops rapidly down the open area into confusing woodlands. Eventually all trails seem to reach the meadow area above the Raghuganga Khola. The route continues to descend to the log bridge stream, then it's up around the bluff on the exposed area. The Raghuganga river below divides in this area into two large flows. Away to the northwest, the main river is seen emerging from a narrow gorge.

Heading mostly down, the trail soon reaches **No-Bridge Stream** meadow and a possible camping spot. For those who continue, there are more uphill sections en route and some slippery downhills. A narrow cliff area is followed by more down, steeply into a stream and out to an open area. This is about 1hr from No-Bridge Stream meadow. The route undulates for a while above the main river, crosses a small landslip, then drops to a large meadow.

Be careful to cross this meadow diagonally to find the small but correct trail down to the lower riverbank. The more obvious path climbs up to some terraced fields with a very dangerous streambank to negotiate. This route does also go to Chhari, but it's much harder. Following the correct trail, the route soon drops to the small dodgy bridge across the Raghuganga Khola, the irrigation channels and **Chhari** (2100m). Say hello but don't touch the nice, noisy doggie!

> **Typical house design**
> Almost all of the houses in the Raghuganga Valley remain traditional structures built in stone, with slate roofs. The lower floor often has a large opening supported by substantial rock pillars. This area is used for storage or to keep animals. The next level often has a shuttered verandah and decorated wooden windows. This is the main living area. Many have an open balconied area facing south for the sun. Big moveable planks are used as shutters. The third floor is often used for spare rooms and storage of more valuable items, including food.

Chhari – Chimkhola (4½–5½hrs)
Chhari – Ghyasikharka – Chimkhola

It's a much easier day from Chhari to Chimkhola. The route is particularly easy to follow after Ghyasikharka, as it's a dirt road. This might be a rather melancholic day as the trek draws to an end – almost, bar the Dragon Cliff cliffhanger!

Once across the bridge from Chhari, the trail follows the riverbank then goes around the hillside to some meadows, home to some inquisitive cows. A few milder ups and downs intervene, but generally it's a pleasant amble in the direction of Ghyasikharka. Just before crossing the Raghuganga, there is a good view of the **two temples** on the west side near Dhar. It's an easy stroll down on the west side of the main river now to the new health post/hospital just before Ghyasikharka.

Ghyasikharka (1864m) is the expected lunch stop, but food or a cook may be difficult to locate. The bridge here across the Raghuganga needs to be crossed; it is not a modern structure. From Chyasikharka the walking is along the virtually unused dirt road, although it starts with a tiring uphill slog to **Kharibot**. Sustenance is possible here, perhaps, if you missed out in Ghyasikharka. Around the next bend mobile phone reception might intrude, with news of the civilised world and much, much else!

Dhaulagiri is on view after a few days' absence. The long and winding road is wide and mostly up with a few junctions. Around a bluff is the concrete kani gate of the

Chimkhola area. This is the **'Chimkhola In Door'** with the 'Dhaulagiri In Door' on the other side. Down the hill are some picturesque traditional houses.

Typical house

In fact it is still quite a long way to Chimkhola (1½hrs). The way descends on the road to cross a landslip area. Across the valley it is possible to see the vast landslide zones north of Rayakhor. These dramatic canyon features of the very deeply gouged Raghuganga Khola are amazing. Eventually a bluff is rounded and Chimkhola comes into view. It's a large village clinging to the hillside with maybe 100–150 dwellings.

Chimkhola (1840m) is the largest community in the greater valley and has a hydro plant, big school, a couple of temples, a couple of 'guesthouses' and communal rubbish bins! It is less than 2hrs from Ghyasikharka. Up through the kani gate is a concrete central plaza with a cute yellow temple. Higher up is the Chimkhola Guest House, with a signboard.

We stayed directly opposite in the **Swadesi Guest House**, although it did not yet have a signboard.

This is the house of Durba Paija, one of the most helpful men one could ever hope to meet in Nepal. Thanks to him and his family for their hospitality, and to Bluetooth for making possible the transfer of his excellent photos from his phone to ours while perched on the end of the bed.

Chimkhola – Dagnam (4–5hrs)
Chimkhola – Darmija – Dagnam

One might expect an easier day, but a couple of side streams and cliffs force the trail to climb around the hillside. At least those cold nights have given way to some warmth; during the day it could be almost too hot. More sweat for the showers in Pokhara!

The trail descends on steps to the dirt road that leads to Beg Khola in the Kali Gandaki valley. This road is so rough that it is only used by tractors (locals told us they prefer to walk!) and is not recommended as an escape route to civilisation. Connected to the school here is the Narjang Computer Hall. Near the school is a suspension bridge donated by the Kadoorie Gurkha foundation of Hong Kong. It takes around 30mins to reach **Sisneri**, where Jirbang, Manapati and then Dhaulagiri appear in all their morning glory. It is quite a steep haul up the road to a corner where the trail for Dagnam begins, about 45mins from Chimkhola.

A staircase leads up to a viewpoint corner which shows off the mountains and the deep canyon of the Raghuganga Khola far below. Now it's steeply down on a staircase that is narrow and a little exposed. Zigzagging down, the way ahead also needs care, before entering woodlands. There is a shortish climb up to a new suspension bridge and a rocky path over the hydro pipe to the first houses of **Darmija** (est. 1850m). The settlement has a number of dwellings, off to the right below the trail, set among hundreds of terraced fields. These will be a riot of green, yellow and gold before the autumn harvest.

Views of Dhaulagiri remain spectacular as the path rises ever upwards into woodland again. Just beyond here, from a porter rest area, three new peaks come into view west of Dhaulagiri. These are Tsaurabong (6395m), Myagdi Matha (6273m) and

Kambon Himal (6570m) – the lower peaks of the Dhaulagiri II and Churen Himal complex. Just a bit beyond here, the mountains take their leave as the trail contours around to the Dragon Cliff, called **Ajingar Bhir** (Veer).

We could describe the next stage as follows – 'now the trail contours along the hillside well above the river!'

Perhaps the description should be left out so as not to give away the excitement of this stage.

The Dragon Cliff legend
Legends say that no man or beast should walk this way until it is light or the first cock has crowed. Anyone straying here in the dark is sure to be eaten by the dragon who dwells in the cliff face. The story is not confined to this cliff, as similar tales abound about dragons in other cliffs, particularly across Dolpo. Eventually the sage Bhimsen came to the cliff and shot his arrows, severing the head of the dragon and saving the people. To this day no one knows whether the headless dragon still lurks in the cliffs.

At first the well-engineered **Dragon cliff** trail is in a wooded area, but soon it twists and turns around the rock faces with a vertical drop on the right. Keep well to the left, especially if passing others coming up, and take care on the steps down.

Further down the path the cliff above is sheer and the cliff below is – well, sheer as well! The trail passes a dragon-like outcrop on the right. Around the next bluff, the path drops even more steeply with an airy view to the right. This really is the ultimate '**airy belvedere**'.

Along the way there is a rather slippery looking stage on the path. The surface of the trail is etched from creamy quartz veins, although it's at least a metre wide, as is most of this trail.

Leaving the cliff and rounding the last bend into the woods, it is possible to appreciate this 'exciting' trail in all its gargantuan or grizzly glory. It is a truly memorable, never-to-be-forgotten grand finale to the trek.

While on the path it is not that apparent just how exposed this cliff area is. If vertigo is your greatest fear in the mountains, then returning the same way to Jhi might be better. For some it's a real buzz and for most it's not that bad really – so long as you don't look down to the right!

From the end of the cliff it is a mere 5min stroll to the jeep park. If you pre-order by phone, a jeep can pick you up here and you can be in Beni within 2hrs. Currently it costs around Rs4000–4500.

Otherwise it is another 20–30mins walk down the road to the village of **Dagnam** (1720m). It claims to have a health post but hopefully none will need to locate it. There are said to be a couple of houses where guests can stay overnight. Jeeps also ply the road to Beni.

It's a sad farewell to the great mountain, the noisy dog and the headless dragon!

Dagnam – Beni (1½–2hrs)
Dagnam – Galeshwar – Beni

As with most jeep rides in Nepal, it's necessary to wait until the springs of the vehicle are flat and the tyres almost touching the bodywork before it will depart. Even when the last person has been bundled in, another may be added for the maximum comfort of the driver's or owner's fat pocket.

As for the rest of the journey, as they always relate on an aircraft – sit back, relax and enjoy the hospitality, and the scenery if you can see it. Beni will seem like paradise after all this – well, maybe not!

Getting to Pokhara is quite possible if the jeep from Dragon Cliff or Dagnam leaves relatively early in the morning. It takes about 5hrs in total of driving time to Pokhara from Dagnam. Pokhara will really seem like paradise – all that food and comfort.

Alternative overnight stops:
South Base Camp – Beni (4–5 days)

This section merely gives a different option for the night stops on the way back to Beni. The itinerary below allows all those who missed out of the great view from Phedi to get a second chance if the weather was bad on the inbound trek. This itinerary also aims to spread the benefits of visitors to other local communities missed on the above routing. It would also be possible to spend the morning in the Sanctuary and then retreat only to Odar. In this case a short day to Phedi could follow, or a longer option down to Chhari. The alternatives are listed in the appendix along with a one-week option trekking only as far as Phedi.

South Base Camp – Phedi (7–8hrs)
South Base Camp – Odar – Phedi

Getting all the way back to Phedi may be possible once the trail is constructed. It might be better to spend the morning in the Sanctuary for further exploration before heading down if the overnight stop is to be **Odar**. Getting to Phedi will be easy in this case the next day. Those who missed the view at Phedi on the way up should choose to stay in Phedi en route to Chhari and Chimkhola.

Phedi – Ghyasikharka (4½–5½hrs)
Phedi – Chhari – Ghyasikharka

This is not such a long day to Ghyasikharka. With more down than up, progress down the Raghuganga Khola is faster, but not by so much. At Ghyasikharka is the **bridge** across to the new dirt road leading to Chimkhola. Homestay options in the village are possible, but during the day many of the people are out in the fields.

Ghyasikharka – Darmija (4–5hrs)
Ghyasikharka – Chimkhola – Darmija

With almost no traffic except a tractor or two, it is more of a steady stroll along a quiet trail. Chimkhola is quite a big settlement. Expect a homestay/guest house or two here and a warm welcome. It is not that demanding getting to Darmija, where the village has overnight options. It would probably also be possible to get to Dagnam on this day if time is limited, but don't stray on to the Dragon Cliff at night.

Darmija – Beni (2hrs + 2hrs)
Darmija – Dragon Cliff – Dagnam – Beni

From Darmija the trail climbs steadily to a great viewpoint of Jirbang, Manapati and Dhaulagiri. Also to the west of Jirbang are the peaks of Tsaurabong, Myagdi Matha and Kambon Himal, part of the Dhaulagiri II and Churen Himal massif. The more demanding stage of the Dragon Cliff follows, but the path is quite wide. Soon after the cliff is the jeep park, but if you need a public vehicle you might need to head on to Dagnam. Getting down to Beni is a bumpy ride lasting about 2hrs.

Alternative: Malika Dhuri Danda (3–4 days)

We did not do this option, but it's mentioned for those wanting a longer trek and a different perspective on Dhaulagiri and Annapurna. The route leaves the Ghyasikharka–Jhi trail near Pakhapani and climbs westwards along the north side of the hills above the Ghopte Khola. Above the headwaters of the river, the trail climbs in thick forest to **Upallo Thadakhani** although it's probably little more than a summer herders' kharka, possibly with a shelter. Further up is another similar place called **Tallo Thadakhani**.

The pass called **Malika Dhur** (3175m) is still higher and is said to offer a view of Dhaulagiri and the Annapurna to the east. We cannot say for sure how good this view is, so perhaps some adventurous trekker who makes it this far can enlighten us.

Descending through forest the route passes **Dichyam** before reaching **Darbang**. From here jeeps ply the dirt road to **Beni** and on to **Pokhara**.

Dhaulagiri Sanctuary Plus Trek

Introduction
Combining the wonders of the Dhaulagiri Sanctuary Trek and the gems of the Kali Gandaki Valley, this trek is sure to arouse attention soon. After the stupendous views of Dhaulagiri from the South Base Camp/Sanctuary, the trek adds in the airy panoramic views from the Ruwachaur Himal ridge. Looking north and east are the ramparts of the Annapurna peaks – Nilgiri, Annapurna I, Fang and Annapurna South. The northern view should take in Dhaulagiri from a closer vantage point, with Tukuche and Dhampus peaks completing the picture. Upper Mustang is glimpsed to the northeast, a vast landscape of brown, red, yellow and grey. Don't expect an easy trail; only woodcutters, herders and itinerants have so far followed this route. Currently **more work is needed on the trail** so we merely outline the future possibilities here.

Planning
There are some specific factors on this trekking route. The altitude will play its role. Ideally the first trekkers should carry ropes and ice axes until the way becomes safer. The altitude gain from Phedi to the pass is around 2000m, so it's no walk in the park. The trail, such as it exists, is very steep with some exposure. The descent to Lete is no easier, with knee-crunching slopes and poor paths that see no maintenance. This is wild forested country where water supplies and flat camping areas are rare. People are even more rare up here; that of course is why some will seek out this pristine environment. Others should definitely keep away and choose an easier option in the Annapurna region.

There is only one way in which to trek in this area and that is with a full camping crew, cooks, porters and extra guides. A local guide is vital to route-finding on this trek. Expect cold weather and be prepared to abandon the pass if it snows. Be sure to get helicopter rescue insurance; this is no place to have an accident without full backup.

Weatherwise it's the same as the Dhaulagiri Sanctuary trek. Watch out for snow that can strike at any time in the spring; in fact it might be better not to plan this trek in spring yet as the trail is not easy to find, even from Phedi. Don't head up here too early in October either or snow will stop this option. Ideally come in November, which consistently offers the most settled spell of weather in Nepal. The trail should be a bit easier to find and follow.

Itinerary and routes

The route is described in the Dhaulagiri Sanctuary Trek as far as the South Base Camp and back to Phedi. It is from here that the fun begins as the path, such as it is, climbs relentlessly to the pass. One might expect to camp below the pass the first day from Phedi in a summer meadow called Pairo Camp. After crossing the first ridge the route climbs yet more to the main ridge of the Ruwachaur Himal. Expect fabulous views for all the effort. Then it is almost all downhill to Lete/Kalopani.

From here the choices begin. The quickest option is the bus to Beni or Pokhara. Others might take a bus to Tatopani, a jeep to Shikha and trek over Ghorepani to Pokhara, either via Birethanti or east to Tadapani, Ghandruk and on to Pokhara.

A harder option would be to follow the steep ascending ridge from Tatopani to the Kopra Ridge (called the Kayer Barah trail) and thence to Ghorepani or Tadapani. Of course some may wish to head north to Jomsom for a flight to Pokhara or on up to Muktinath. Also in future there might be part of the Annapurna North Base Camp trek on offer via the Thulobugin ridges.

Dhaulagiri Sanctuary Plus Trek Summary	
Start	**Beni** (830m)
Finish	**Lete** (2480m)
Distance	approx. 52–60km (33–38 miles)
Time	14–16+ days
Maximum altitude	**Ruwachaur Pass** (4500m/14,760ft)
Trekking style	Lodges, homestay plus camping
Transport	Bus, jeep and plane

Dhaulagiri Sanctuary Plus Trek Profile

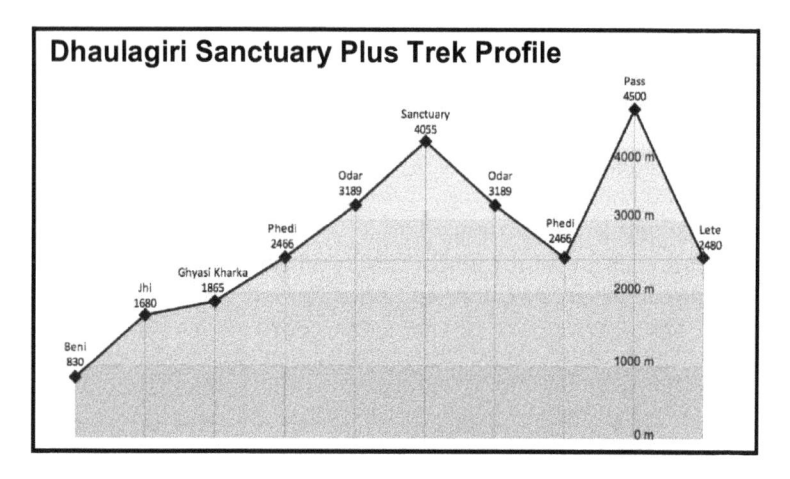

Kathmandu – Pokhara (30mins or 6–8hrs)

The choice is between a long but scenic bus journey on the busy road via Mugling, or an often-delayed domestic flight. This sounds far too negative for a guidebook. Sorry! Either way, the excitement is generally positive.

Pokhara – Jhi (3–4 + 1–2hrs)
Pokhara – Beni – Kushma – Jhi

Jhi – Dhaulagiri Sanctuary (4–6 days)
Jhi – Ghyasikharka – Odar Camp – South Base Camp

Dhaulagiri Sanctuary – Phedi (7–8hrs)
South Base Camp – Odar Camp – Phedi

See the route descriptions above under the Dhaulagiri Sanctuary Trek

Phedi – Pairo Kharka (6–8hrs)
Phedi – Pairo Kharka

A fear of steep trails may not be the best attribute today as it's a formidable climb. The trail hides in the forest for most of the day and there is little view. Of course the forest has its own attractions: silent glades, moss-covered deadwood, lichen and eerie pockets of damp undergrowth. There is little respite from the severe upward direction and the sun barely makes its mark on the path. Take a packed lunch and a thermos of hot water, as there are few water sources en route. The camp may change with the seasons. **Pairo Kharka camp** is estimated to be around 3700m, above the treeline in open meadows.

Typical tangled forest trail with fallen trees

Pairo Kharka – Forest Camp (7–9hrs)
Pairo Kharka – Ruwachaur Ridge pass – Forest Camp

Another day and another big climb as the route continues now above the trees. As far as we know, the trail is vague up here but heads northeast.

Eventually the route climbs up to the Ruwachaur Himal ridge pass (est 4500m) and suddenly a panoramic view opens out. Behind is the Dhaulagiri massif and, if not here, fairly soon to the east, the great walls of Nilgiri, Annapurna I, Fang (Shikha Barah) and Annapurna South should be in view. The never-ending descent continues northeast and it would seem that the route is rugged and ill-defined. Once back in trees for the rest of the day, it's down and down to a forest camp (est 3600m).

Forest Camp – Lete/Kalopani (7–9hrs)
Forest Camp – Lete/Kalopani

Again the trail is in forest, with a few isolated open areas. Gradually the descent edges across to the more obvious valley of the Lete Khola. After a seemingly endless descent, the path gives glimpses of the Kali Gandaki valley far below, and the villages of Kalopani, Larjung to the north and further beyond, Tukuche.

The last stage is down into the Kali Gandaki valley close to the Lete Khola. Just north of the point where the trail joins the main Annapurna Circuit route at Lete is Kalopani (2530m). This is the only place on the whole Annapurna Circuit from where the elusive Annapurna I peak can be sighted; it's mind-blowing at sunset.

Lete has a few lodges, although better ones are found up the trail in Kalopani.

Annapurna I and Fang from Kalopani

Of course it's now possible to take road transport all the way from Kalopani back to Pokhara. However, those with time can enjoy the east bank trail down to Tatopani and even walk on over Ghorepani and by various options down to Pokhara. Even more adventurous is the Thulobugin Ridge option that will eventually be part of the future Annapurna North Base Camp Trek.

Lete/Kalopani – Dana (7–8hrs)
Lete/Kalopani – Ghasa – Dana

Following the road is much quicker and the volume of traffic is still light, but taking the alternative marked trail is not to be missed. Currently there are few good facilities along the trail, except basic lodgings in Pairothapla and Kopchepani, so be aware of your timings and don't get caught out in the bush.

Coming from lower Kalopani, the trail is easily located but from Lete it's not so obvious. The trail in the forest of pines is serenely peaceful– it's an entrancing walk. The trail drops into fields to a junction. Dhaulagiri and Tukuche Peak are stunning from here. Continue on and look for a boulder painted with signs – Ghasa is ahead and Lete right.

Continuing the trail comes to a farmhouse and junction. Turn right into the forest, ignoring a vague path to the left. The village of **Chhoyo** is visible across the main river. Soon you rejoin the main road (1hr).

ACAP has already constructed a new trail from Chhoyo to Ghasa, although it has suffered from landslides so check if it's open. This avoids the road, passing through quiet forest and open countryside above the vast landslide seen from the road lower down. It does have a short section of exposure along cliffs.

Having followed the road, now south of Lete, for less than 10mins, look for a trail steeply off down to the left – oddly, it's not marked by ACAP. The road does a long loop northwards towards Dhaulagiri so descend to the bridge and climb steeply back up to the road.

About 2hrs from Kalopani you reach the teahouse of **Ghumaone**, where it's best to follow the road briefly. **Kaiku** (2085m) is the first part of Ghasa, so follow the road to the path, left into the main part of Ghasa (2010m). This is the last of the Thakali villages, with some picturesque houses, a small monastery of the Nyingmapa sect and good lodges.

The checkpost men will be waiting to pounce here.

The trek is now in the deepest part of the Kali Gandaki gorge and towering cliffs dominate the landscape. Join the main road near the bus depot and continue to the lower area of Ghasa, with more lodges. Continue on the road for a few minutes to a sign indicating Tatopani to the left across the suspension bridge – a trail you should take to avoid the road. It is marked in red/white here. Incidentally the next escape point to the main road is not until near Kopchepani, leading across to Rupse Chhara.

Once across the Kali Gandaki, the path is narrow and heads into wooded areas and spindly bamboo. It undulates and climbs up around the hillside with a great view of the road below. Eventually the trail descends to **Pairothapla** (1890m), 1hr from Ghasa, with one basic lodge. Continue up through the village and then lose height in the scrubby forest. The trail climbs around a small landslide before making a steep descent to the fields of **Kopchepani** (1620m).

Follow the trail to the left and climb steeply with views of the dramatic Rupse waterfall across the valley. A sign indicates, 'To Tatopani' and 'Way to Gadpar' (Gadpak). Climb to a small shed-like building. This is a traditional animistic shrine with Shaman-style, morbid-looking fetishes outside.

With views of Dana ahead continue down quite steeply, with care, to **Gadpar**. It's not far now to the suspension bridge leading to **Dana** (1400m) and the main road. **Dana** is right, off the road, up into a quaint old street decked out with flowers, lined by beautiful old merchants' houses and a few reasonable lodges.

Dana – Tatopani (2–3hrs)
Dana – Tatopani

There are two options from here: head through Dana across the bridge and follow the road to Tatopani, or take the trail via the Mristi Khola. The famous Mristi (Miristi) Khola was the gateway to Annapurna I for Maurice Herzog's French expedition in 1950.

The Mristi Khola trail crosses back over the Kali Gandaki and goes right along the riverbank on a muddy section. There is a junction soon, go right, then shortly go left uphill following the red/white markers. Now it's a super walk along the riverside in rainforest, serenaded by the ever-harmonic cicadas.

The marked path climbs up steps with a brief exposed bit above the river to **Sharap**. Just beyond the village is a mini-hydro plant. Cross a small concrete bridge and at the junction go right. Ignore the suspension bridge over the Kali Gandaki. Continuing around the cliffs the route undulates before a final descent to the mysterious gorge of the **Mristi Khola**. There is a hint of Barah Shikha (Fang) in the sky above but, as ever, Annapurna I is hiding her face.

Cross the Mristi Khola and reach a school with a sad-looking temple nearby. The obvious route heads down to the suspension bridge across to the road. **Tatopani** (1190m) is close and has some pleasant lodges with gardens. The hot springs have long been a magnet for sore feet and aching bones.

Buses for Beni leave when overfull and rarely pick up people en route. A jeep road via Shikha has shortened the trek up to Ghorepani, another option.

Dana street view

Dhaulagiri Circuit Trek

Introduction
The Dhaulagiri Circuit Trek is for some one of the best mountain treks in Nepal. It has all the right ingredients. The lower trails from Beni are a kaleidoscope of village life in the foothills, with picturesque farms, traditional villages, rice-terraced hillsides and enchanting woodlands. Higher up trekkers enter the world of ice and snow; the trails creep close to glaciers and the peaks soar to preposterous heights. The trek is not for the faint-hearted, with glacier walking and two high altitude passes above 5000m. Those with mountaineering experience might relish the challenges, but all must be well prepared, including the Nepalese support crew.

Planning
Although there are lodges in the Kali Gandaki valley and limited offerings along the lower Myagdi Khola, the basic trek requires a full high altitude camping crew. The main headache on this trek is the need to camp in the dip (Hidden Valley) between the two high passes – French Pass (5360m) and Dhampus Pass (5305m). Any issues with altitude here are serious; there is no way to go down to a lower height. A helicopter rescue might be the only recourse. This means it's absolutely vital to be fully acclimatised before French Col, meaning added cold nights around Italian Camp, Glacier Camp and Dhaulagiri Base Camp. In these high areas there is always a risk of avalanches and being caught in bad weather.

Ideally all trekkers here should be well versed in the use of ice axes and crampons. For those with little mountaineering experience, most groups are provided with training on the use of mountaineering equipment. These basic skills will be required for crossing the two high passes.

Weather aspects have to be considered seriously. These days it's not beyond the realms of possibility to get a weather forecast from one of those 'Weather Gurus' mentioned in the Sorcerer of the Clouds box.

Itinerary and routes

The usual itinerary for a trek around Dhaulagiri takes 19–20 days, depending on the route from Marpha to Pokhara. The road from Pokhara to Beni is OK and now dirt tracks lead from there via Darbang to Muna. It should be possible to start trekking from around Phaliyagaon before Muna, but in case the jeeps or the road are not functioning, plenty of time should be allowed when planning the itinerary.

We have not done much of the route and rely on notes from HMH, Ade Summers and Roland Hunter of the Mountain Company for more detail. Only a brief outline is given here. The trek follows the Myagdi Khola for most of the approach from Darbang through Dharapani, Muri (Mudi), Naura, Boghara, Lipsaba, Dobang and Sallaghari (Chaur Bag). Be sure to do the trek with a well-equipped and experienced operator. Itineraries and route suggestions are given in the appendix.

Dhaulagiri Circuit Trek Summary	
Start	**Darbang** (1110m)
Finish	**Marpha** (2670m)
Distance	approx.130–140km (82–88 miles)
Time	19–21 days
Maximum altitude	**French Pass** (5360m/17,580ft)
Trekking style	Camping with some lodges
Transport	Bus, jeep, plane, helicopter!

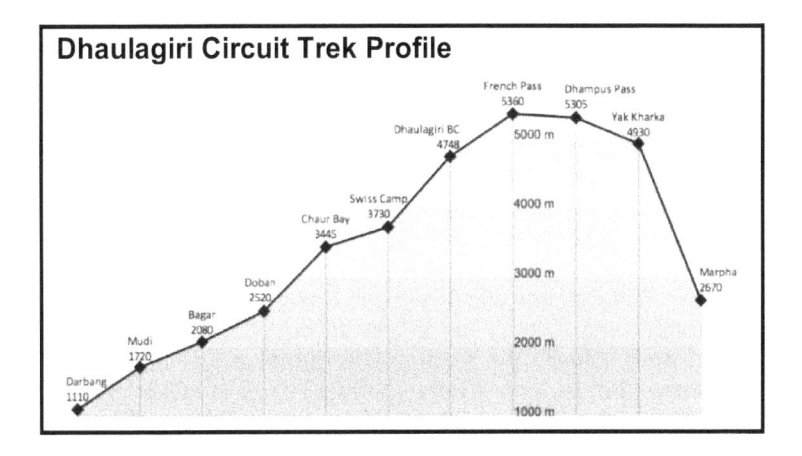

Dhaulagiri Circuit Trek Profile

Darbang 1110, Mudi 1720, Bagar 2080, Doban 2520, Chaur Bay 3445, Swiss Camp 3730, Dhaulagiri BC 4748, French Pass 5360, Dhampus Pass 5305, Yak Kharka 4930, Marpha 2670

The following itinerary is the usual route taken by most groups. Be sure to check that sufficient acclimatisation days are included in any itinerary presented when planning.

Kathmandu – Pokhara

Take the flight, or 'ease' into the routines on the bus journey to Pokhara. Eat up – it's the last chance for a right royal banquet!

Pokhara – Babiyachaur/Darbang (6–10hrs)
Pokhara – Beni – Tatopani – Babiyachaur/Darbang

The trek begins with an exciting journey from Pokhara to Beni and Darbang (Darbanga). The road is pretty good these days as far as Beni, so that at least is a blessing. The jeep road onwards is not such a gift, with rough and at times head-bumping sections.

Following the Myagdi Khola valley, the route climbs gently through **Tatopani** (985m) and on to **Babiyachaur** (970m), which depending on the road conditions might be as far as it's possible to get this day. If lady luck is smiling, then continue to the main roadhead at **Darbang** (1110m). It's generally quite a warm journey in these lower climes for much of the season, in stark contrast to what lies ahead.

Darbang – Dharapani (3–4 hrs)
Darbang – Dharapani

With ever more dirt road construction across Nepal, this might be the latest stage to succumb to the dusty wheels of rickety Indian-made jeeps – they are actually good robust vehicles these days, at least when they are new! If walking is necessary or preferred, allow 6hrs.

Unless Babiyachaur was the overnight stop, today is a short walk. Initially the route is along the Myagdi Khola before climbing the spur after the Dang Khola. It takes 3hrs or so from Darbang to reach **Dharapani**, a typical Gurung village. Gurja Himal is in view from close to Dharapani.

Dharapani – Muri (5–6hrs)
Dharapani – Phaliyagaon – Muri

The rough dirt road apparently now goes almost to Muri so there could be a choice of walking or 'jeeping'. Following the trail, the route goes through Takam and Sibang, where the many terraced fields are used to grow mainly rice and wheat.

If the road is used, the trekking now starts at **Phaliyagaon** (1850m), just before **Muna**. It should be possible to start trekking on this day, but as already emphasised allow extra time for when planning in case of delays on the poor dirt road. The trail descends to cross the Dar Khola and straight away climbs into the now much narrower Myagdi Khola valley that runs from north to south here.

The uphill continues to a small pass (1807m) before the Magar village of **Muri** (also called **Mudi**) (1720m). Along the route there should be glimpses of Gurja Himal and Puta Hiunchuli towards the west.

Muri – Boghara (6–7hrs)
Muri – Naura – Boghara

It's a day of mixed interests, with farms, villages and some wooded country. The valley is increasingly hemmed in as the slopes are ever steeper.

From Muri there is a steep descent to the bridge over the Muri Khola. The relatively easy trail continues through bamboo strands and various clearings with fields and farmhouses through **Mahatala** (1575m) to **Naura** (1570m). Further north the valley sides are steeper and the trail is exposed in places. Continuing along the Myagdi Khola, the trail climbs steadily around and on to **Boghara** (also called **Bagar** at 2080m).

Boghara – Dobang (6–7hrs)
Boghara – Lipsaba – Pitangkos Kharka – Dobang

The countryside is increasingly remote as the route climbs into wilder country. The places marked on the map are little but shelters used by herders.

From Boghara the trail is along the west bank of Myagdi Khola, in forest. The trail is rarely even remotely level for more than a few minutes. **Jeltung** (1880m) is the last settlement in the valley. Higher up the hot spring on the way might make for a refreshing break and a feeling of cleanliness (even saintliness!). Then it's onwards and upwards fairly easily to **Lipsaba** (1970m). The cliffs high above the trail host the bees' nests of the 'honey hunters' made so famous by Eric Valli. En route is the Hire Khola waterfall and **Pitangkos Kharka**, where little happens apart from summer herding. Higher up is **Dobang**, also marked on the maps as **Doban Kharka** (2520m). It's a pleasant spot in the forest with several basic teahouses and a campsite. At this altitude the nights are getting colder. You may need to carry warm clothing for the cold afternoon.

Dobang – Sallaghari (5–6hrs)
Doban Kharka – Chaur Bag/Sallaghari

It's a tough day, as the trail climbs 900m and more. The ambience is changing; in this 'throne of nature' nothing manmade stirs. To the east of the trail are the soaring ramparts of the peaks of Jirbang and Manapati.

The valley narrows and the trail continues in wet, dense cloud forest with ferns, bamboo clumps and rhododendrons in evidence. There will be few views on offer and virtually no human presence. The route crosses to the east bank of the Myagdi Khola on a new cantilever bridge. It's a bit of a teaser, the last stretch up around the **Talitre Khola** side stream to **Chaur Bag/Sallaghari** (3445m) in a forest clearing; *chaur* means small meadow. High above are the snowfields and glaciers of the Manapati-Dhaulagiri southwest ridge.

Sallaghari – Italian Camp (3–4 hrs)
Sallaghari – Puchar Base Camp – Italian Camp

Again the trail continues to climb. Only the rustling of nature's creatures disturbs the eerie silence. The trail climbs into beguiling pine trees, with more stunted rhododendron and birch. Once above the tree line, heather, juniper and azaleas are more common.

The route climbs ever higher through **Puchar Base Camp,** which has been destroyed by a landslide. As the names suggest, these spots were chosen as base camps by various expeditions in the early days of climbing the peak. Then it's on to a grassy area and then a lateral moraine where **American Camp** and **Italian Camp** (3660m) are located.

High above camp is the impressive west face of Dhaulagiri with the peak of Tsaurabong (6395m) to the west. Snow can carpet these high spaces at any time.

Rest day: Acclimatisation at Italian Camp

Being the highest camp of the route so far, it is necessary to spend a day acclimatising to the new altitude. After the rigours of the climb and the tangled path in the forest, most will appreciate a day of doing nothing much here.

Italian Camp – Glacier Camp (5–6hrs)
Italian Camp – Chhongardan Gorge – Glacier Camp

The raw mountain ambience can be daunting, as the trail cuts its way ever higher. Already the noise of creaking glaciers fills the air and in the 'narrow gorge' the noise of tumbling rockfall is a little disturbing! Some groups take helmets for this stage, such is the risk of missile attack.

From Italian Base Camp the trail descends steeply down the lateral moraine to access the glacier. Sometimes it is necessary to use a fixed rope here. In the narrow gorge near the **Swiss** and **French Camps** the going is tough, especially if there is fresh snow.

The route now is across the glacier and then along the moraine on the left side of the impressively narrow **Chhongardan** (also spelt Chonbarden) **gorge** to the snout of the **Chhongardan glacier**.

It's another hour via the so-called **Japanese Camp** (3890m) to **Glacier Camp** (4200m), where a few ledges have been levelled in the ice for tents. The altitude is beginning to bite here, as well as the bitter night temperatures. Dhaulagiri (8167m) looms dramatically above the camp on the east side.

Route to Glacier Camp (photo: Ade Summers)

Rest day: Acclimatisation at Glacier Camp

Due to the extreme altitude gain to Dhaulagiri Base Camp, most groups have an acclimatisation day at **Glacier Camp** near the Chhongardan Glacier.

There is an optional side trip from here up the glacier towards Base Camp to a large **moraine ridge** with views of Tukuche, Little Eiger, the icefall from the Northeast Col plus the valley heading towards French Pass. This morning side trip might take around 4hrs.

Some mountaineering experience is handy for extra exploration.

Glacier Camp – Dhaulagiri B.C. (5–6hrs)
Glacier Camp – Dhaulagiri B.C

At these altitudes, the slightest incline upwards starts to feel like a chore. However, the mountain scenery is some of the most spectacular in the Nepal Himalaya and at such close quarters.

The trail climbs on a rough trail along the moraine-covered glacier where the odd crevasse could be encountered. The steady but exhausting climb continues to **Dhaulagiri Base Camp** (4710m) and a winter wonderland of glacial ice and snow. From here it is the northwest face of Dhaulagiri I that shines out. Also in view are Tukuche Peak, the Little Eiger, and further to the west, Dhaulagiri II (7751m) and Dhaulagiri IV (7618m).

Camping below Dhaulagiri (photo: Ade Summers)

Rest day: Acclimatisation at Dhaulagiri B.C.

With the certainty that escaping from Hidden Valley if altitude strikes is not likely, it's best to be cautious and plan on an extra day here too. The whole ambience of the location is so overpowering that this day will be one of the most memorable parts of the high mountain experience. For amusement and to aid acclimatisation, it's worthwhile to climb towards French Pass. Basic mountaineering skills will be required for crossing the high passes.

Dhaulagiri B.C. – Hidden Valley (7–8hrs)
Dhaulagiri B.C. – French Pass – Hidden Valley

This is a day of superlatives, at least as far as the scenery goes. With a very slow, tiring, long ascent, it's a tough call getting across the Ooh La La pass, more commonly known as French Pass. Already Dhaulagiri is well to the south and Tukuche Peak looms large to the southeast of the pass.

From Base Camp the route is along the moraine and over to the left hand side of the Upper **Chhongardan glacier**. It is necessary to gain the high lateral moraine ridge visible further up the valley by following a steep trail across the scree and talus. From the lateral moraine ridge, there are superb views of Tukuche Peak and Dhaulagiri I back down the valley. A large cairn on the lateral moraine ridge marks the turn off to the final ascent of the pass. The last climb is across an easy-angled snow slope to **French Pass** (5360m), topped by prayer flags and cairns. Ooh la la!

On the pass (photo: Ade Summers)

At the pass a sense of achievement is at hand – hopefully! It's the highest point successfully conquered on the whole trek. There are superb views of Sita Chuchura, the peaks of the Mukut Himal, Tashikang, Tukuche Peak and, naturally, of Dhaulagiri I. In this euphoric state, take care on the moderate snow slopes and quite long descent to the **Hidden Valley** (5050m or on the map 5244m)! The camp is next to a river not far from the base of Dhampus Peak, but only isolated patches of moss and grass are found this high; it's in the rain shadow of the main Himalayan peaks.

Sunset and sunrise in the snowy bowl are stupendous. Hidden Valley slopes off to the north, a mysterious place below the Sandachhe Himal that lures the adventurous in the extreme.

> **The joys of Hidden Valley**
> Some parties have a day off in Hidden Valley to explore a ridge on its western side. There are views of Dhaulagiri, the Nilgiri peaks, the Annapurna summits and down Hidden Valley towards Sandachhe Himal. Others groups have a pre-arranged (with climbing permits) attempt on Dhampus Peak (6060m). This is only for those with previous mountaineering experience. An early start is advised, since there is an altitude gain of over 1,000m from Hidden Valley at 5,050m to the summit at 6,060m. Depending on the conditions, the route ascends on moderate snow slopes and scree along a ridge to the summit. There's a sensational view of Dhaulagiri, the Annapurna peaks and into Mustang.

Hidden Valley – Yak Kharka (8–11hrs)
Hidden Valley – Dhampus Pass – Yak Kharka

Getting much sleep in Hidden Valley is a tall order, with bitter temperatures and restlessness induced by altitude. Having mastered the highest pass, the day dawns with renewed anticipation. However, this is a long day, by far the hardest on the entire Dhaulagiri Circuit trek, especially in snow.

The climb is again extremely tiring, but mainly up moderate snow slopes to **Dhampus Pass** (5305m). The views are rewarding, mostly of Dhampus Peak and the fluting of Tukuche Peak. The descent is not at all simple, as the trail contours around high in the snowfields before making much downward motion.

From the pass the trail descends for about 100m before starting to traverse left into the Kali Gandaki valley. Crampons may be needed for the next stage, depending on the snow conditions (including for the porters). It's a very long traverse on snow, often taking 4–7hrs.

There are stunning views of Nilgiri and the western end of the Annapurna Massif on this traverse. After this is the final steep descent to **Yak Kharka** (est 4800m).

Yak Kharka – Alu Bari (1½–3hrs)
Yak Kharka – Alu Bari

A knee-crunching drop continues from here, but the views east remain mesmerising for most of the day. The gradient is quite demanding, but getting down to Marpha is often done.

The descent continues to **Alu Bari** (3900m) but it is a much easier trek down now. The more arid nature of the Kali Gandaki valley far below is apparent from here, with pine forest still below the camp. Those pushed for time may descend all the way to Marpha, but that means around 2200m of steep descent in one day.

Whether this is possible will depend on if you are fitter after the pass or knackered with bad knees, and whether you have a plane to catch!

Alu Bari – Marpha/Jomsom (2½–4hrs+ 1hr)
Alu Bari – Marpha/Jomsom

The brutal descent continues. At the end of the trek the welcoming sight of **Marpha** (2670m), with its temptations of apple brandy and apricot 'wine', is enough to wash away all the knee aches – hopefully.

Be sure to visit the Buddhist sights of Marpha. If you are planning to fly from **Jomsom** to Pokhara, a jeep ride takes from 15mins or so. Those wanting to walk or take a bus might head on down along the Kali Gandaki to **Tukuche**, a super place to restore the energy.

Jomsom – Pokhara (30mins flight)

This is certainly the easiest and quickest way to reach Pokhara, but be aware that the flight may be cancelled if the wind is too strong or the clouds too low. If this happens, it should still be possible to get to Pokhara later the same day, as the fights are usually early in the morning. It's not the most fun-filled trip in one day though, so if that does not appeal, allow an extra day for the road journey.

Alternative: Marpha – Pokhara (1–2 days)
Marpha – Tukuche – Kalopani – Beni – Pokhara

Buses and some jeeps depart from Marpha for the lowlands, and a mellow journey ensues as the accomplishments of the trek sink in. The last sight on offer is that of the Dhaulagiri Icefall. Long ago some believed that a way beside this gigantic ice chute might lead to the conquest of Dhaulagiri. Of course, as mentioned above, it's possible to get to Pokhara in one long, grinding haul from Marpha, but it may be too sudden an end for most. The trek back via Kalopani, Tatopani, Ghorepani and Ghandrung could take another week.

Dhaulagiri Icefall

Dhaulagiri Icefall
High above the Kali Gandaki and below the east face of Dhaulagiri is one of the most impressive glaciers in the region. Although a much-talked-about route, the trail to the Dhaulagiri Icefall is not well marked. One route begins near Larjung. A number of trekkers have been lost and have disappeared on this route, even very recently. It's vital to be well equipped and go with a local guide.

Ghasa village entry gate

Dhaulagiri Dolpo Trek

Introduction
This trek packs its punches in quick succession and is ideal for those with weeks to spend in the western regions. Lucky those who can contemplate such a big extravaganza of a trek – this really is a full circuit of the Dhaulagiri massif in the extreme. On a clear day, the arc of peaks stretches from Kanjiroba in the west through Churen Himal and Putha Himal to the towering peak of Dhaulagiri and its adjacent satellite spires. Later the full grandeur of the Annapurna range opens out, with Tilicho, Nilgiri, Annapurna I, Fang and Annapurna South – enough to satisfy the most ambitious mountain lover.

The only way to reach Dolpo before the advent of the motor road west from Pokhara was to walk all the way via Beni and Dhorpatan over the Jang La pass to Tarakot. This essentially was the route taken by Peter Matthiessen and George Schaller in their search for the snow leopard and themselves. This extended trek holds so many exciting possibilities. Taking in eastern Dolpo, the scenery could not be more of a contrast to the middle hill approach. Wild, arid country and high passes with panoramic views across the region are inspirational. Choices abound as the routes to the Kali Gandaki to the east hold yet more breathtaking scenery. Culturally this trek is a winner, all the way from the Hindu lowlands to the Buddhist mountain zone.

Planning
Trekking the whole circuit has one big advantage; it cuts out all those unpredictable elements associated with flying in Nepal, allowing one to plan more accurately a complete but very long trek into and out of Dolpo. Of course taking the flight from Jomsom to Pokhara at the end is a possibility.

A guide is necessary, since few foreigners come this way and, if you want to savour the scenery in comfort, you need to add a cook and a few porters into the equation. Fully supported camping is the main option so far, but adventurous independent hikers will be able to find very basic lodges and homestays if only going as far as Dunai.

With a number of high passes en route, it's never entirely predictable when the best weather will prevail. As a rule, the best time of year for viewing the sweeping panoramas across most of Nepal is mid-October through to mid-December. For most of Nepal, March to mid-May is fine, but here March and even early April is too early, with snow on the passes.

That said, crossing the high passes in Dolpo is more of an issue. Normally these are best done before the end of October/early November. Locals usually head down to the warmer areas for winter, often as early as late October. This means the trek along the southern flanks of Churen Himal to Tarakot (in late September and early October) is not going to be at the best time. Generally the regions west of Pokhara do not get the disturbed weather that afflicts the central and eastern mountains earlier in October. Later spring and into May is also possible, but views may be hazy and the lower valleys quite hot. Nothing is certain these days, though.

Itinerary and routes
Today it's possible to reach Beni in a few hours by the mostly sealed road. A jeep track extends west almost as far as Lulang to Muna via Darbang and should continue to be pushed westwards. Within the life of this guide, the dirt road should reach Dhorpatan. It's anyone's guess how far west it might get, since unsealed routes continue to push well into the high mountains with surprising rapidity. Not far west and north of Lulang is the Gurja region, where new trekking routes have been developed. Beyond this and below Gurja Himal peak the trail continues west under Churen Himal. After the Putha Himal the route crosses the Jang La pass to Dunai and Tarakot. For more comprehensive details of the route as far as Tarakot, see the Himalayan Map House guide to the Guerrilla Trek by Alonzo Lyons, who was accompanied by travel writer Surendra Rana.

From Tarakot most trekkers head up the Tarap Khola to Dho Tarap, a traditional Dolpo village. Then the tough bit starts, with a climb over the Jhyarkoi La into the upper Panzang valley. Across the Mo La is the exotic outpost village of Chharka Bhot. Wild and remote country follows to the Jungben La, then it's on to Kagbeni and Jomsom. Another option is to head east from Dunai along the little-visited

Bharbung Khola and into the Mukut valley. Here some mountaineering experience is required to cross the Mukut La to join the first option before the Jungben La. A third, even wilder, option could be to head north and east from Chharka along the Chharka Tulsi valley and over the Ghami La pass into Upper Mustang.

Itineraries and route suggestions are given in the appendix. The following itinerary is the most popular route. We have not done the first stage between Beni and Tarakot, so the notes are necessarily brief. Approximate timings from HMH sources are shown in the appendix. See the maps at the back of the book.

Dhaulagiri Dolpo Trek Summary	
Start	**Darbang** (1110m)
Finish	**Jomsom** (2720m)
Distance	approx. 240–260km (150–163 miles)
Time	28–29 days
Maximum altitude	**Jungben La** (5550m/18,200ft)
Trekking style	Camping with some lodges
Transport	Bus, jeep and maybe plane

Kathmandu – Tarakot (13–14 days)
Kathmandu – Pokhara – Beni – Dhorpatan – Tarakot

Take the flight or ease into the routines on the bus journey to Pokhara. The trek begins with the exciting journey from Pokhara to Beni and Darbang (Darbanga). The road should be pretty good these days as far as Beni after rebuilding works – that at least is a blessing. The jeep road onwards is not such a gift, with rough and at times head-bumping sections.

From Darbang the dirt road leaves the Myagdi Khola valley heading to **Dharapani** and on to **Takam** (1675m). (The Myagdi Khola valley leads to Dhaulagiri Base Camp and the circuit via French Pass to Tukuche.) After Takam the way is through to **Sibang** to **Muna**, where the road ends for now. After **Lulang** (2470m) is the little-visited Gurja Himal region. This lies to the north of the usual trail to Tarakot and can be explored from Gurjakhani. From Lulang and **Moreni** (2280m) the trail crosses the **Jaljala pass** (3415m), where high meadows offer views before reaching the Uttar Ganga River. A night can be spent in **Gurjaghat** (3015m), with simple accommodation on offer.

A shorter hike from Gurjaghat heads to **Chhentung**. A rare Bon monastery is found nearby, with an associated medical school. Beyond here is the **Dhorpatan Hunting Reserve** known for its superb pristine forests. A fee is apparently collected here for trekkers, but hunters must, of course, fork out much more for the privilege of pursuing various permitted species. **Dhorpatan** (2870m) was almost taken over in the 1960s by a mass of Tibetan exiles. It's a small place in a fertile valley and has a small airfield that was used in the 1970s–80s, but flights seem to have been discontinued these days.

From Dhorpatan the route heads to **Thankur** (3175m), another long day of up to 8–9hrs. Heading northwest, the landscape becomes more open, similar to the Scottish highlands. The normal trail heads through **Syal Pake** to a small pass known as **Kukur (Dog's) Pass** (3000m) and on to **Phalgum Pass** (3920m), now well above the tree line. Magnificent views are promised from here when the weather cooperates.

This region is often referred to as Rukum district and the people are known as Kham; their language is very different from Nepali. Their picturesque houses have flat roofs. **Kayam** (3000m) is the next settlement, with basic accommodation, and then the trek continues to **Pelma** (2425m). Pelma is noted for its church and a bridge that was famed for its erotic carvings. A trail leads directly from Pelma towards Dolpo, but it is exposed and generally avoided. In any case, taking the longer but easier route via **Maikot** (2300m) adds cultural interest to the route. Maikot is an appealing traditional village with elegant houses and lively Magar culture.

From here the trail continues to **Dhule** (3410m) above the Pani Dal Khola, and then heads northeast, keeping to a high ridge. The views are fabulous. Then the route drops into the **Sen Khola valley**, a paradise for naturalists, to **Phuphal Phedi** (3940m). This route is marked on more recent maps as the 'Yarsagumba Trail'. Further on is **Purbang** (4065m).

The final obstacle to trekkers approaching Dolpo this way is the infamous Jang La pass, so well described by Peter Matthiessen and feared by many for its snowstorms. The **Jang La** (4535m) is a formidable climb, but soon afterwards the way drops into more pleasant climes.

Ahead lie the hidden lands of Dolpo. One trail heads to **Dunai** and another to the ancient fortress town of **Tarakot**, once the capital of the Tichurong kingdom.

Tarakot
Tarakot has always been a trading crossroads and was once the capital of an independent kingdom called Tichurong, meaning fragrant waters. Sitting high above the raging waters of the Thulo Bheri, the settlement once had a dominating fortress. One of the more illustrious items traded through Tarakot (and Jumla and Dunai) was musk. These days that trade is far less. To the south the only access to Tarakot is across the infamous Jang La pass, the first break in the defences west of the great barrier of Dhaulagiri and Churen Himal. Many of the Magars of Tarakot are Buddhist.

Tarakot – Laina Odar (4–5hrs)
Tarakot – Laisicap – Laina Odar

The route ascends significantly today, at first along the Thulo Bheri River, then skirts the Bharbung Khola and finally heads up the Tarap Khola. As the trail meanders around the bend of the Bheri River, the vegetation starts to become less lush; replaced by the increasingly drier hills.

Leaving Tarakot, the trail is on the south bank of the Bheri River and within 2hrs needs to negotiate the large side valley of the **Bharbung Khola**. The path heads across the Bharbung Khola and on well-engineered steps to **Laisicap** village (2775m), where basic homestay is a possibility.

The trail then crosses the main river and continues north around the spur, staying on the west side of the Tarap Khola until the substantial village of

Kanigaon. Across the valley Chhedhul (Sandul) Gompa can be seen. A steep and tiring section continues up to **Laina Odar** (3375m) with a notable waterfall. Large temporary tents can be used for rough overnights here.

A basic lodge is likely to open within the lifetime of this guide, but don't rely on this.

The myth of Gumbatara (Digong Gompa)
by Jag Budha

Digong Gompa was founded by Lama Nagpo Jumne in the 13th century. Nowadays this is a community gompa, located at the top of Tarakot village. It takes 1½hrs to reach there from Tarakot campsite. Many years ago a Tibetan lama, Nagpo Jumne, was sent by his guru to find a place with an elephant-shaped village. He travelled through Upper Dolpo continuously, walking for many long weeks, but did not find anywhere answering that description. After more long days of walking he reached Tichurong, but still did not find any elephant-shaped village. So he continued to walk along the Bheri River. When he reached Byasghar, a fly bit him from behind. He turned round to swat the fly and immediately saw a village shaped like an elephant's shoulder. He studied it intensely and realised it was just as his guru had told him. Finally he returned to that place, nowadays known as Gumbatara village, but whose old name is Digong Gompa. When he reached there he found the centre of village occupied by a Milky Lake; around the edges of the Milky Lake were the village households.

Laina Odar – Toltol (7–9hrs)
Laina Odar – Chhyugar – Toltol

The route continues its dramatic way ahead, forging on through deep gorges and threatening-looking cliffs. It's another long walk, but the tantalising, snaking path keeps its secrets throughout the day, slipping in a surprise here and there.

Within 2hrs of leaving Laina Odar heading north, the trail is exposed. Blasting has improved the route in sections, where logs and flat slates had been used to defy nature's original grand designs. **Chhyugar** (3440m) has a camping spot overlooked by demon-faced cliffs. The narrow defile of the river dominated by sheer-sided ghostly crags seemingly bars the way.

After crossing to the west bank, the small settlement of **Nawarpani/Pibuk** (3475m) is the next place of note. **Toltol** (3523m) is a couple of hours further on.

Toltol – Dho Tarap (6–8hrs)
Toltol – Ghyamghar – Langa – Dho Tarap

The geology is strikingly exposed for all to see along the valley; sometimes it threatens to show a new face, where landslips are inevitable.

The path continues on the northwest bank to **Ghyamghar** (3755m) with a cave above and a small monastery that is unlikely to be open. The trail crosses to the east bank. At **Sisaul** the path crosses to the west bank to avoid the less inviting cliffs. Sometimes the sheer walls threaten to cut off the way ahead.

Beyond **Langa** the trail is bereft of settlements and it's surprisingly lonely. After a small rise the path descends to **Dho Tarap** (3944m).

Dho Tarap, Ribo Bumpa monastery

According to ancient legends, the valley of Dho Tarap was once a vast lake (tso) inhabited by a spirit. One day a horse (ta) appeared from the lake; it was seen to be a horse of great quality (rap) and hence the place became known as Tarap. Dho Tarap has distinctive chortens and a magnificent monastery picturesquely located above the houses. Dho has a few not-so-cheap lodges. Batteries can be charged and horses can be hired.

> **Ribo Bumpa Monastery**
> Located high above Dho Tarap, this is one of the most important gompas in Dolpo. It was built by Jigme Nyima Gyaltzen and Lama Tenzin Targye around 1000 years ago, supposedly being constructed to ward off evil spirits roaming the place. Local legend refers to Guru Rinpoche and it is said that any damage to this gompa will cause Phoksundo Lake to burst and flood the villages. The name Bumpa relates to the vase, one of eight sacred symbols of Buddhism. There are three large Bumpa here, cast in pottery symbolising the original chortens. Inside are the central 3m high Guru Rinpoche plus eight of his other aspects, including Dorje Drollo. The three Buddhas of the past (Dipankar), present (Sakyamuni) and future (Maitreya) are prominent, as is the thousand-armed, eleven-headed Chenresig. Various Yab-Yum male-female images are on show, including the impressive Samantabhadra on the right of the main door. On the west wall is a Green Tara plus Namduse, the money deity, with a mongoose in attendance. The medical practitioner and Amchi, Dr Namgyal Rinpoche, has been the abbot since 1994 and has assisted with the publication of Dolpo: The Hidden Land produced by SNV, and published in French by Himalayan Map House.

Dho Tarap – Upper Panzang Camp (6–8hrs)
Dho Tarap – Dhoro – Upper Panzang Camp

There are two different routes to Chharka Bhot from Dho Tarap. The southern route crosses the Chan La pass, but is generally shunned by locals (no reasons were given, but it seems to suffer from heavier snowfalls and the canyon sides look unstable). The northern route over the Jhyarkoi La (5360m) is a hard pass, but the following Mo La (5030m) is an easy passage, making this the preferred option for trekkers as well. In any case, it gives a glimpse of the upper Panzang valley. There's no sustenance en route, so at breakfast you'll have to have your fill of tsampa – needs must. Less than an hour from Dho Tarap are the Dhoro and Shipchok monasteries, which could be visited on a half-day outing from Dho, as the Jhyarkoi pass is a long, brutal day. Allow 3 hrs for the sightseeing trip.

Dhoro Monastery

The Dhoro monastery is a small Nyingma-pa edifice and, if you're heading east, is the last Buddhist shrine until Chharka Bhot. It takes less than 1hr from Dho Tarap to reach here. Getting into the gompa is problematic as there are usually just goat herders about; we got lucky. The goats may be hiding the key to the monastery, so ask around. It is locally called Nyima Phug Gompa.

The main image of importance is Tsepame (Amitabha). Across the walls there are some faded 1000-Buddha images. The south wall has an excellent protector image of Mahakala. Other icons are Guru Rinpoche, Green Tara, Vajrasattva in front of the altar and one local idol, Sengge Muka. Dhoro village has but seven houses and children have to trek up to the Crystal Mountain School for their education.

Heading east from lower Dho Tarap, the path follows the north bank of the Tahari Khola. Avoid the upper trail or you will visit the remains of a much-depleted structure and face a small canyon before Dhoro. The trail heads up to the small, red tin-roofed monastery of **Dhoro**.

Across the river before Dhoro to the south is **Shipchok**, home to a Bon monastery with an impressive series of chortens. A bridge spans the river, so there's no need to wash your feet here.

From Dhoro the trail soon turns left into a starkly brutal, sheer-sided canyon. The settlement of **Maran** is little but fields and pasture. The trail is more than a little exposed, with vertiginous drops on the left side. However, the sheer grandeur of the canyon's grey, ochre, red and brown colours wipes away any angst about impending doom.

Shipchok (Sipchhog) Monastery

Sipchhog means 'sheltered place' and so it is, located in the quiet Mirbu side valley adjacent to the main route to Chharka. This not-to-be-missed Bon gompa was founded about 500 years ago, although it is likely that its original birth was 800 years back. Triten (Treton) Chime is reputedly the original founder. The old monastery probably fell into decline when the Bon established a major centre at Phoksundo. It was under Yungdrung Gyaltzen that this gompa was rebuilt. Inside is the image of Tonpa Shenrap, the founder of the Bon. Other images are Namgyal and Jamma, an affectionate goddess. There are some 1000 Buddha-like images. Apparently the texts here include 'The Magnificent Pure Teaching' and the Bon text 'To Fight against Malevolent Spirits'. When Snellgrove visited, he noted Bon paintings of Tonpa Shenrap, Satrig, the sky god Ganachakra and the Nyingma-pa master Guru Rinpoche. On the entry chamber walls are some mandalas and decorative diagrams. Three carved lion heads grace the lintels and there are four guardians. Outside are 15 chortens set in an arc across the meadows, with one isolated smaller chorten by the fields.

A vast sandy yellow-coloured valley opens to the west, a haven for bharal, blue sheep. The path heads up between two streams to a shelf, a possible campsite. Further up is another dry gulch camp where water is some way down. By now it dawns on the trekker that the pass is not ahead towards the snowy col, but to the left up the immense, sheer, loose face below the rocky summit outcrops. This horrendous climb is the steepest of the passes described so far. It soon became known by us not as the Jhyarkoi La but as the **Frigging La!**

The stumbling climb takes all of 1–1½hrs and it's the 'toe-licking' steepness that is to blame. A false summit is the reward for all this toil. The **Jhyarkoi La** (5360m) is won and the prize is the bitter cold of the swirling frosty winds. And the views... they are m-ma-mag-magnificent. To the south, towering snowy peaks and icy ridges dominate the views. Looking north, just a short walk down from the top, the valleys are rolling and brown – the **Panzang Valley.**

The descent is relatively easy once away from the loose upper area and that devilish wind. Looking east, the flat-topped snowfield of the **Kirphuk ridge** turns a brilliant red in the twilight, enough to guide the way down to the undulating pasture. There are various flattish spots for **camp**.

Upper Panzang Camp – Chharka (5–7hrs)
Upper Panzang Camp – Mo La – Chharka Bhot

The wild country walk continues across the Mo La (5030m). The main settlement of Chharka Bhot (previously spelt Tsharka) is the only settlement of any note in the entire valley. Beware of agitated dogs in this forbidding-looking place; few foreign devils pass this way.

Leaving camp, the trail curves up around the hillside, heading southeast. Far across the valley yaks graze, pretending to be oblivious of any human presence. The climb is steady and not taxing as the gradient is friendly. There are icy streams to cross and small gullies out of the wind. Through a series of humps and hillocks, the path winds around to the huge summit cairn of the **Mo La** (5030m).

Again the 'topside' is buffeted by the frigid wind. The climb takes around 2–3hrs. **Churen Himal** peeps out to the south and, looking east, the country is rugged and very uncompromising. Chharka is hidden below the folds of the descent. The descent is easy as the trail creeps in and out, passing mani walls and scrubby bush. However a **deep ravine** blocks the way and it is necessary to edge down on loose material into a streambed and immediately begin a tiring but brief climb. An hour later the ancient, three-tiered kani gate of **Chharka Bhot** (4302m) is at hand. Chharka's main claim to fame is as the village seen at the beginning of Eric Valli's Caravan/Himalaya film. The name means 'good salt', Chha – Ka, since locally mined crystals were of much sought-after quality.

Looking like a fortified citadel, the houses are intricately bound together with few windows. Narrow alleys with excitable children and curious adults lend flavour to the vision. Numerous chortens dot the area. Down across a new steel suspension bridge are a surprising number of lodges. Residents suggest that the winter exodus from Chharka begins around 15 November. Only the very young, infirm, sick trekkers and anyone caught without rupees or spare dollars will be left here to endure the snow-encrusted winter nights.

Typical houses in fortified Chharka

Sarchhen Monastery, Chharka

> **Sarchhen Monastery**
> This Nyingma-pa gompa dates back over 700 years and was built by Sagar Rabjam. It's the only monastery in the Chharka valley. A kindly old lady let us in to see the basic offerings. Five images rest above the altar, including Guru Rinpoche. Two donors flank the great Tantric sage, with books and a couple of thangkas. Externally the building is simple but it commands a great view over the village. Sit and wait for a while outside if you can't get in; you will be spotted and someone may arrive with the key.

Chharka – Nulungsumda Kharka (8–10hrs)
Chharka – Tulsi – Nulungsumda Kharka

Leaving Chharka Bhot, the trail strikes east into uninhabited wild country. The isolation just adds to the feeling of being somewhere the world has forgotten. The very long day involves a steady gain in altitude. Camps also exist along the valley before Nulungsumda Kharka (4987m) if it gets too long!

Leaving Chharka the trail goes east, passing mani walls, below dry cliffs. After 30mins the route crosses a fine bridge to the south bank. Inevitably the trail needs to climb and it does so to a prayer flag. Then it contours up and down to a suspension bridge (2hrs). There immediately follows a punishing ascent through turrets of sandstone conglomerate draping the cliff. The spectacular trail is loose, steep, nearly sheer in places and extremely dusty. Around here is the **Tulsi Khola** that drains the hills west of Upper Mustang and the trail across the Ghami La pass.

Once above the ghostly turrets, the trail turns south into the Thasan Khola that only just allows passage to Nulungsumda. The path meanders uphill across meadows and icy streams. Rather more relentlessly, it continues going ever higher.

An exciting, exposed section follows, where the path has been carved out of the cliff and the route follows the east riverbank, sometimes on stepping-stones in the water. Almost 3hrs from the turret climb is the confluence with the **Yalku Khola.** From here the countryside opens into a wide plain below high, barren hills and snow-dusted peaks.

Abundant herds of yak, who never seem to breathe heavily, make light of this wild country. It's an interminable walk across this plain, but slowly the valley narrows. The wind is funnelled into this wide area, making the afternoon a bitter pill to swallow.

Various other camps can be found if **Nulungsumda** cannot be reached.

Nulungsumda – Ghalden Ghuldun (6–8hrs)
Nulungsumda – Niwas La – Jungben La – Ghalden

The approach to the Jungben La pass (5550m) is notoriously windy, so it is vital to wear adequate clothing and wrap up with a scarf. It's a day of serious 'highs' in terms of prolonged altitude. Remember your torch and spare batteries in case the day is longer than planned. Nulungsumda is a walled kharka where the trails divide – east for the Jungben La and south for the Mukut La. (This southern route heads for the Mukut Himal and the Bharbung Khola valley down to Tarakot – an inviting prospect for a few hardy trekkers perhaps. It is a 5–6hr **side trip** to the **Mukut La**. See description in reverse later.)

The trail climbs easily to the **Niwas La** (5120m), not a true pass but a window on to a broad plain dominated by stunning snow-drenched peaks of the Sandachhe Himal. The most prominent peak is **Tashikang** (6385m). The trail keeps to the north side of the valley. To the south is a fantastic chasm where sandstone bands hold treasures like herds of blue sheep and ancient caves. This deep, narrow, impassable canyon links to the **Hidden Valley** below French Pass on the Dhaulagiri Circuit Trek.

The ascent of the Jungben La begins with a long traverse but is not that steep. About 3–4hrs from camp, the pass is bagged. The **Jungben La** (5550m) offers an utterly stunning panorama to the east. Straight ahead is the Thorong Pass with the Chulu peaks behind it. To its left is Upper Mustang, including the amazing Narsing Khola canyon and the Damodar Himal.

Dhaulagiri II from Jungben La climb

View east from the Jungben La pass

A steep but short descent leads into the barren, empty valley of the Lhanhimar Khola. There is a nasty icy stream to cross here, with no bridge. Beside the stream the trail on the north bank heads east for 30–40mins to a small col wrapped by jagged rocks and prayer flags. Once more the panoramic view is breathtaking and so is the very serious descent below. Take extreme care – the path is loose and knee-jerking as it zigzags endlessly downwards.

An intermediate stage takes 20mins to a promontory. From here the tortuous path drops down, across yet more loose chips of slate and shale. The views are still fabulous, but stop before you look around!

The trail darts briefly left to a flat spot and then over the lip down to **Ghalden Ghuldun Camp** (4247m). There's nothing here but a flattish spot and a juniper tree or two.

Ghalden – Santa (4–5hrs)
Ghalden – Kyalunpa Khola Bridge – Santa

With the snow peaks of the Sandachhe ridge dominant to the south, the trail dips and dives across the arid, deeply incised canyons of the Kyalunpa Khola to Santa (Sangdak of old). Although Santa is seen below, it takes most of the day to reach its terraced fields.

From Ghalden camp the trail drops down sandy ridges. A great sheer wall of loose sandstone and mud towers over the shelves that characterise this walk. The path is loose and steep. It takes 45mins to reach the suspension bridge across the **Kyalunpa Khola** and the last stage is extremely exposed but photogenic.

Immediately the climb begins out of the windblown chasm; hold on to your hats on the bridge. The trail contours high above the river, now lost from sight. It is narrow and exposed in places, but evidently widened. Continuing up, the trail eventually reaches a high point near some intriguing organ pipe features.

Soon the way drops to a shady juniper tree, ideal for lunch, about 3hrs from camp. From here the path remains difficult in places, with a few more ascents but generally contouring downwards.

Santa (3777m) is a small, almost ghostly, village with tiny alleys, straw storage sheds and only a few houses. In winter many Santa residents go to Ghok, where conditions are less harsh. Watching over the cluster is the open-roofed village inn, a teahouse that no one could really call a place to stay.

> The sherpas sleep crowded in one corner of the teahouse like a cluster of hibernating marmots.
> *Stones of Silence*, **George Schaller**

Santa – Kagbeni (8–9hrs)
Santa – Bhima Lojun La – Tirigaon – Kagbeni

The final day of the trek takes the weary trekker down into the relatively busy highways of the Mustang region and the Kali Gandaki valley. However, first a big slog over the Bhima Lojun pass is in order.

Leaving Santa, the trail assaults the hill immediately behind the village, a rather sudden, steep uphill first thing in the morning! About 1hr of this climb is required to reach the ridge **top cairn.** From here the route is more forgiving, as it eases into a side bowl.

Be careful to take the uphill trail before coming to a landslide on the level trail. Two water pipes are dangling in space here and climbing around the slip is dangerous. The next ridgeline – another false summit – is about 2hrs from Santa and yet again another side bowl has to be negotiated. After this it's a short rise to the **Bhima Lojun La** pass (4450m). The view is sensational again. Far to the north is Upper Mustang in its near entirety. East is that old favourite, the Narsing canyon, backed by the Damodar peaks.

South and east are the Thorong La, the Muktinath Himal ridge, Annapurna III, Gangapurna, Roc Noir and the Grand Barrier, Tilicho Peak, Annapurna I, Nilgiri and Barah Shikha (Fang).

Heading down it's a 1600m descent; the trail is steep but relatively OK with only brief exposed areas. Quite soon silver birch and juniper make an appearance, heralding warmer climes. The herders' sheds at **Yak Kharka** are eventually encountered near a man-made pond used by mules. The red **monastery of Tirigaon** appears on a bluff far below. The rim of the Kali Gandaki valley is down here with the final zig-'sagging' drop to the riverbank (about 3hrs from the pass). Suddenly the trek is nearly over. **Tirigaon** is 15mins north; allow 1hr to take in the monastery or stay overnight.

Kagbeni (2810m) is a mere 15mins south along the river. The delights of ancient Kagbeni are well known, with its citadel and mysterious alleys, but modern Kagbeni has better lodges, cafés and means of communication!

Kagbeni – Jomsom (3hrs)
Kagbeni – Jomsom

These days, jeeps depart Kagbeni around 9am for Jomsom. Taking less than 1hr, they rattle down past those who choose to walk in 3hrs. The Bon monastery of Lubra is up a side valley to the east, near Eklebhatti. The jeeps park at the north end of Jomsom, so it's necessary to walk through the long town to all the tourist facilities at the south end near the airstrip, banks and hotels etc.

Jomsom – Pokhara
Jomsom – Ghasa – Beni – Pokhara

From Jomsom there are flights to Pokhara. There are buses to Ghasa, taking 2½hrs. At Ghasa the Annapurna Conservation Area Permit needs to be shown and then after a while another bus departs from Ghasa to Beni, taking 3–4hrs. From Beni to Pokhara take a jeep, taking 3hrs.

Alternative: Tarakot – Jungben La via Mukut

The Bharbung Khola valley leads eastwards below Putha Hiunchuli, Churen Himal and the lesser peaks of Dhaulagiri to Mukut. This unexplored valley sees virtually no trekkers, but its mysteries must be well worth the effort. As a fabulous exit route, hardy trekkers can cross the Mukut La to a point above Nulungsumda, between Chharka and the Jungben La pass. From the Mukut La it's a relatively short but tricky and icy descent to near Nulungsumda. We have not done the route and it's only added here for those with **significant mountaineering experience** looking to find an offbeat route. With no lodges, it is a fully supported camping trek. Be sure to ask around for a guide who lives in the region in Dunai or ask Explore Dolpo in Kathmandu; www.exploredolpotrekking.com

Mukut Himal (right) & Dhaulagiri II (behind centre)

The route begins from Tarakot to **Laisicap** and then goes east along, and often high above, the Bharbung Khola. After **Tachingaon** there are no settlements until **Kakkotgaon**, where the river does a sharp dogleg through a canyon.

On the north bank now, the trail climbs high above the river through the small outposts of **Pimarigaon** and **Chinan** before contouring around to **Gharengaon**. Somewhere below here it will be necessary to cross the Bharbung Khola.

A less well-used trail climbs up the Mukut Khola to the settlement of Mukutgaon. Towering above the whole valley here are Dhaulagiri II (7751m), Sita Churchura (6611m) and Mukut Himal (6087m). From Mukutgaon the route follows the valley up towards the Mula Tal lake before diverting north across the **Mukut La** (est 5650m).

The descent follows the **Malung Khola** valley down to **Nulungsumda Kharka** (4987m) and the trail via the Jungben La to **Kagbeni** and **Jomsom**.

187

Dhaulagiri Kopra Panorama Trek

Introduction
Quite a popular trek, the Dhaulagiri Kopra Panorama Trek is better known as the Annapurna – Dhaulagiri Trek. Although within the Annapurna Conservation Area, the trek actually gives some of the best views of Dhaulagiri from its high and wild ridge viewpoint of Kopra. The trail through the forest up to the high meadows tends to be less busy than most, making the approach to Kopra a pleasant and beguiling experience. Climbing up the ridge from Kopra towards Annapurna South and Khairetal Lake is sensational, although laced with risk if there is heavy snow. It is not actually necessary to reach the lake to appreciate the fabulous views of Dhaulagiri, though.

Planning
Apart from mild altitude effects, the main issue on this trek has always been the abundant snowfall. The ridge is exposed in places and snow makes this worse, sometimes to the point of preventing any advance to the lake. There definitely is a slight risk of slipping off the trail on one stage. Snow can strike at any time in the spring; don't head up here too early in October either.

With lodge development north beyond Tadapani, the trek is rarely experienced as a fully supported camping expedition nowadays. Those heading for the pilgrimage lake of Khairetal and up into the higher country below Annapurna South still need to camp. It's worth adding a day on Kopra Ridge in case of heavy snowfall.

Lodges and homestays are possible in Meshar, Isharu, Dobaato, Bayeli, Chistibung, on the Kopra Danda ridge and in the village of Swanta.

Itinerary and routes
There are various ways in which to organise the trek. Some following the traditional route begin from Dhampus or Australian Camp and head via Pothana and Deurali to Landruk. Then a big descent to the Modi Khola follows before an even bigger ascent to Ghandruk. These days many trekkers cut this stage by taking transport to Naya Phul and

jeeps along the Modi Khola as far as possible towards Ghandruk. From here it's a pleasant climb to Tadapani and then the trails become wilder northwards to Kopra.

The absolute minimum timeframe for the trek from Pokhara is 9 days, assuming the route begins near Ghandruk, avoids any diversion up the Kopra ridge and descends immediately from Ghorepani to Birethanti/Naya Phul for Pokhara. A more balanced and relaxing approach would take 10–12 days.

Dhaulagiri Kopra Panorama Trek Summary	
Start	**Dhampus** (1650m)
Finish	**Naya Phul** (1070m)
Distance	approx.70–80km (44–50 miles)
Time	10–12 days
Maximum altitude	**Khairetal Lake** (4200m/13,780ft)
Trekking style	Lodges, homestay and camping
Transport	Bus, jeep or taxi

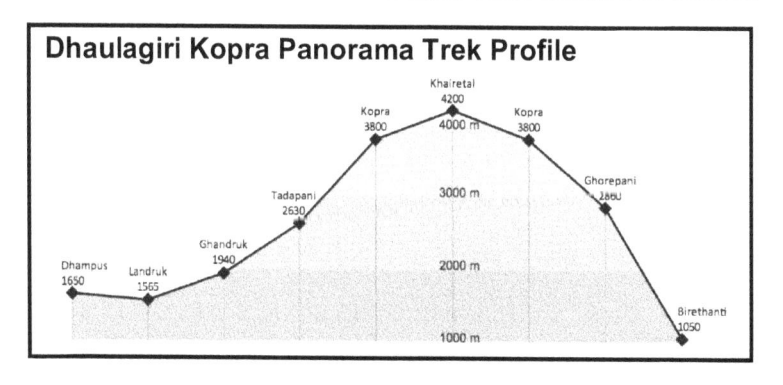

Dhaulagiri Kopra Panorama Trek Profile

Kathmandu – Pokhara (30mins or 6–8hrs)
Kathmandu – Mugling – Pokhara

Take your choice of transport.

Pokhara – Dhampus (2hrs+ drive)
Pokhara – Dhampus Phedi – Dhampus

The road heads out of Pokhara along the Seti River valley passing Tibetan refugee centres to fast growing Hyenja. Soon after is the less smooth road up from Dhampus Phedi to the ridgetop village of Dhampus. Some new quite luxurious lodges can be found along the ridge.

Dhampus – Landruk (5–6hrs)
Dhampus – Pothana – Tolka – Landruk

Once upon a time this was a busy, popular trail, before roads were carved into the hillsides. The scenery remains spectacular, despite the modern intrusions.

From **Dhampus** (1650m), the route climbs around and up to **Pothana** (1890m). Not far up is **Deurali** (2100m) and then it's down through eerie forest to Bheri Kharka. The trail drops further and once clear of the trees heads around the bowl to **Tolka** (1700m). The final short contouring route leads on to **Landruk** (1565m).

Views of Annapurna South and Hiunchuli at sunset are spectacular.

Landruk – Tadapani (6–7hrs)
Landruk – Ghandruk – Tadapani

As the Himalayan Griffon flies, the distance between Landruk and Ghandruk across the Modi Khola valley is little, but the trail is a teaser.

Barely before you've put your boots on, the path plunges steeply down and down to the **Modi Khola Bridge**.

Watch for the 'honey hunters' in the canyon. The altitude gain to Ghandruk is more than the descent and it's a hot, sweaty climb!

Ghandruk (1940m) is a 'must see' attraction with its old village, a tightly woven network of slate-roofed houses and alleys. However, don't linger too long or it will be dark on the last climb to Tadapani through the enchanted forest.

The enclave of **Tadapani** (2590m) is a cosy spot, but at night this eerie haunt seems to be alive with all the beasts of the forests.

Ghandruk village below Annapurna South

Tadapani – Dobaato (5–6hrs)
Tadapani – Dobaato

Breaking away from the main trail here, the route is northwards through thick forest and highland scrub reminiscent of the Scottish moors. This trail has no obvious destination for anyone except trekkers and hunters.

From **Tadapani** the morning's hike is through cool, damp forests following a herders' and woodcutters' path. There is little sunlight but some amazing exotic plants and trees – rhododendron, magnolia and a myriad of orchids. Being a quiet trail, there may be a lot of bird life here.

Be careful navigating among the twisted roots and gnarled trees. Apparently new basic accommodation is found at Meshar and Isharu en route. The afternoon walk is once again in thinning forest with a few significant ups and downs to **Dobaato** (3420m), where a good new homestay/community lodge has been developed. Mist may hide the snowy summits of Annapurna South, Machhapuchhre and the distant Himalchuli in the afternoon. At dawn they sparkle brightly; that's pushing one's luck saying that!

Dobaato – Chistibung (3–4hrs)
Dobaato – Bayeli – Chistibung

It makes a wonderful change to be trekking so close to nature. With so few people on this trail, the wildlife is less wary, giving quiet trekkers a chance to see the shy creatures of the forest.

The route continues through remote wilderness in the shadow of the lower ramparts of Annapurna South (7219m). At Bayeli there is a community lodge. En route are isolated bhattis (basic dwellings), where wild-eyed, roughly dressed men cut wood while others herd their goats on the meadows.

Chistibung (3000m), just below Dharamdanda, is the usual night's stop, being little more than a few terraces, a couple of houses and two new lodges.

Chistibung – Kopra Danda (3–4hrs)
Chistibung – Kopra Danda

The chill of a misty dawn soon burns off and the distant peaks gain in clarity. The trail climbs and descends almost disconcertingly; the path is sometimes muddy underfoot. The seemingly never-ending final climb to Kopra Ridge is quite demanding.

From Chistibung the route contours around the vast hillside high above the Kholang Khola. It then drops into the densely forested upper reaches of the Dhasta Khore Khola with its complex network of tributaries and gullies. Far below, the deep ravines and damp canyons are disturbed only by the echoing sounds of screeching birds.

After a daunting descent, the trail makes a determined effort to gain height via a long and taxing climb; the top is always just a bit further. And so it goes on, with some anticipation of the views to come.

One cannot fail to be moved by the staggering vista from the Kopra Danda (about 3800m). There is now a community lodge here. Lammergeyers, Himalayan Griffons, vultures, eagles and other large raptors often circle above the ridge.

Dhaulagiri at sunset from the Kopra Danda

Be sure to stay at Kopra for sunset. Long before the last rays of sunlight desert Dhaulagiri, the sensational colours of dusk are amazing: hazy blue tints, jet-black couloirs, silvery cornices, and dazzling white snow painted in glorious shades of pink and red.

Darkening bluish shadows in the deepest gorge on earth between Annapurna I and Dhaulagiri grow longer while millions of stars twinkle above Nilgiri, Tukuche Peak and their companions on the Tibetan border.

It's a magical sight.

Kopra – Khairetal Lake (8–10hrs)
Kopra – Khairetal Lake

Getting all the way to the lake and back in one very long day is done by some trekkers, but 'normal' walkers do it in 2 days. This of course creates a problem, as there is a need to camp out for one night. According to the latest reports, tents are available in Kopra and there has been talk of making a shelter/lodge. The intermediate campsites vary according to the availability of water and the season. Because of deep snow, we have twice failed to make it to the lake in the past (giving a 65% chance of success).

Annapurna South from snowy Kopra

At dawn, as mist obscures the valleys, a sweeping panorama of floating Himalayan giants appears: Churen Himal, Dhaulagiri, Tukuche Peak, Dhampus Peak, the Upper Mustang peaks, the Nilgiris, Annapurna I, Fang and Annapurna South. The Kali Gandaki Valley is far below.

Countless hazy blue ridges stretch as far as the eye can discern towards the Indian border.

The route basically climbs steadily all the way, with the tantalising peaks of Annapurna South and Fang periodically screened by the rocky outcrops. Given a clear path, getting to the isolated pilgrimage lake of Khairetal and the Barah shrine (4200m) is rarely insurmountable, so long as you are well acclimatised. Expect a long day, start early and take a good torch. Don't forget warm clothing in case the descent is late.

Khairetal / Khayer Barah Lake
Khairetal Lake is holy to Hindus, who come here for the Janai Purnima festival in August (a difficult expedition at that time of year, with monsoon leeches and muddy trails). Dramatic cliffs surround the beautiful, tranquil waters – it is a remarkable place of great serenity, where only the squawking of predatory eagles and vultures pierces the silence. It is not hard to understand how this spot became a significant religious pilgrimage site.

Khairetal Lake

Take great care retracing your steps, descending the occasionally exposed ridge. The panoramic vistas along this hairy belvedere are spectacular in all directions, so the distractions are magnificent but beware!

Kopra Danda – Ghorepani (6–7hrs)
Kopra Danda – Swanta – Chitre – Ghorepani

A tinge of sadness is felt on leaving this lofty viewpoint, but there is a certain attraction in reaching the warm climes of

Chitre, far, far below. The surprise of the day is just how far down Chitre actually is, particularly since it is easily in view for most of the day. Ideally allow two days to reach Ghorepani.

Views of Fang, Annapurna South & Hiunchuli

The trail drops very steeply from the ridge towards the distant bright yellow mustard-filled terraces. Stop for a moment to admire the view of Ghorepani, Poon Hill and the old mule route snaking down towards the Kali Gandaki Valley. The trail is knee-crunchingly relentless to the small fields and houses of Swanta (Soweta).

Eventually, after scrambling down the tumbling trail to those once seemingly tiny fields, the route joins the main trail at **Chitre** (2390m).

From there it's a big pull back uphill, but soon enough it's time to celebrate the day and nightlife in the mountain metropolis of **Ghorepani** (2850m).

Ghorepani – Naya Phul (7–9hrs)
Ghorepani – Ulleri – Tirkhedunga – Naya Phul

Having bagged such a great view from Kopra, you may not be inclined to take on Poon Hill. But if you do have any reserves of energy, don't miss it; add a day, overnight in Tirkhedunga.

From Ghorepani the trail snakes down to **Banthanti** (2300m), with views of Machhapuchhre. **Ulleri** is a good place to have a lunch break before the knee-exercising drop on hundreds of stone steps to sunny **Tirkhedunga** (1540m). Lower down in **Hille** (1475m) it's almost too warm. Too hot, too cold – some people are never satisfied. Lovely buses, cranky jeeps or super-fast taxis run to Pokhara from **Naya Phul**.

Dhaulagiri from Poon Hill

Machhapuchhre near Ghandrung

Parbat Myagdi Treks

Southwest of Poon Hill and Ghorepani is an area of great potential for those trekkers seeking to leave the crowded trails behind. The developing Parbat Myagdi region, also known as the Mohare Danda Trek, sits on hillsides facing west and northwest, with outstanding views of Dhaulagiri. With quiet, rural pastoral scenes and virgin forests, this new trekking area has a series of good village-based homestays and community lodges. Jeep roads may shorten some itineraries. Having an experienced local guide is definitely necessary. Route-finding through settlements, across hillsides and in forests is difficult with so many junctions and trails; the wild forests are certainly not places in which to be alone.

One option is to access the area from Phalante (near Chitre) on the main trail between Tatopani and Ghorepani, and walk down to meet the Tatopani–Beni–Pokhara road. Although not currently marked on the maps, a trail also links these homestay villages with Poon Hill. See Parbat Myagdi Link Trek.

You can also do a circular trek without going into the Annapurna Conservation Area (at the moment, at least) by following this 7–8 day itinerary: Pokhara to Beni and Galeshwar, then on foot to Ghumaone–Banskhara–Danda Khetri–Nangi–Mohare Danda–Tikot–Tiplyang and then back to Beni along the road. See Parbat Myagdi Circular Trek. Times and descriptions are estimated for guidance only, as we have not done these routes.

Parbat Myagdi Link Trek

Parbat Myagdi Link Trek Summary	
Start	**Phalante** (2300m)
Finish	**Galeshwar** (1020m)
Distance	24km
Time	4–5 days, various options
Maximum altitude	**Nakako Bisaune** (2990m: 9807ft)
Trekking style	Homestay & lodges
Transport	Bus, jeep, taxi

Phalante – Mohare Danda (6–7hrs)
Phalante – Nakako Bisaune – Mohare Danda

Starting near **Phalante** (2300m), the trail climbs up generally southwest for 1hr or so to cross a ridge at **Nakako Bisaune** (approx 2990m). It then contours to a community lodge at Danda Kharka before making the climb to the **Mohare Danda** ridge (3225m), an exciting viewpoint, with a stunning vision of Machhapuchhre. Much of the way is through forest of pine, rhododendron and chilaune trees. Keep a lookout for birds such as the White Owl, Himali Kokale, Nyauli and Dundul. Fleet-of-foot wildlife includes deer, fox and the elusive leopard.

Mohare Danda – Nangi (3–4hrs)
Mohare Danda – Nangi

From Mohare Danda the way heads down to Nangi (2300m), a Magar village which has homestays plus a typical oval-shaped community structure for schoolteachers and visiting volunteers; see www.himanchal.org. **Nangi (Nagi)** was noted as the 'internet village' in the early days of the internet because of its enterprising locals and international donors. Oranges grow on the warm, sunny hillsides surrounding the village, which also has a small temple. There are good views of Dhaulagiri and Churen Himal.

Nangi – Danda Kateri (2–3hrs)
Nangi – Danda Kateri

For a shorter trek down the next day, you may overnight in the settlement of **Danda Kateri** (2009m), with a community dining hall and homestay options. The Pyari Barah temple is near here.

Danda Kateri – Banskhara (2hrs)
Danda Kateri – Banskhara

Some 800m below Mohare Danda is another Magar village called Banskhara (1526m), with more homestays.

Banskhara – Galeshwar (1–2hrs)
Banskhara – Galeshwar

The descent to Ghumaone Tal is relatively short but quite steep. Galeshwar (1020m) is 15mins downstream along the road to Beni and expanding rapidly. It's worth a break to see the temple – a large complex built on a mound of rock. There are a couple of reasonable lodges in Galeshwar near the suspension bridge on the north side.

Parbat Myagdi Circular Trek

Parbat Myagdi Circular Trek Summary	
Start	Galeshwar (1020m)
Finish	Tiplyang (1040m: 3410ft)
Distance	33km (21miles)
Time	7–8 days, various options
Maximum altitude	Nakako Bisaune (2990m: 9807ft)
Trekking style	Homestay
Transport	Bus, jeep, taxi

Galeshwar – Banskhara (2hrs)
Galeshwar – Banskhara

To avoid all the main trails and do this as a circular trek, start near Galeshwar. Cross the Kali Gandaki at the Ghumaone bridge and trek up to Banskhara (1526m).

Banskhara – Danda Kateri (2–3hrs)
Banskhara – Danda Kateri

Continue uphill to Danda Kateri (2009m). Homestay is possible here.

Danda Kateri – Nangi (2–3hrs)
Danda Kateri – Nangi

It's pretty much all uphill through farms and isolated woods to Nangi (2300m), the once famed 'internet' village.

Nangi – Mohare Danda (4–5hrs)
Nangi – Mohare Danda

The trail climbs ever higher into the beautiful forests that characterise the upper slopes of Poon Hill. Continue to Mohare Danda (3225m), an exciting newly discovered panoramic viewpoint.

Mohare Danda – Tikot (6–7hrs)
Mohare Danda – Tikot

Since we are unfamiliar with the trail, we can only assume that, mostly, it contours around the hills and then drops down to Tikot (approx 2200m).

Tikot – Tiplyang (2–3hrs)
Tikot – Tiplyang

With a bigger descent today to the Kali Gandaki valley floor, the trail zigzags down around the cliffs to Tiplyang (1040m) and then back to **Beni** and **Pokhara** along the road.

****

Apparently, homestays are also being opened in the villages of Khiwang and Swat, both on the hillside west of Shikha. Khiwang is quite a large settlement with around 800 inhabitants, while Swat has roughly 50 houses. The people here are known locally as the Pun Magar.

Look for a new route called the **Karbakeli Trek** in this area in future.

Gurja Himal Treks

Introduction
It would be fair to say that hardly any trekkers have been to the area below Gurja Himal. The main peak on view from here is Gurja Himal (7193m), which forms part of the Churen Himal ridgeline west of Dhaulagiri. Being remote, the area has retained some incredible cultural aspects. The main village is Gurjakhani and from here a series of short routes branch in all directions, including northwest to Churen Himal Base Camp. Gurjakhani is also known as the Hidden Village. The whole region is famed for the mining activities that once brought prosperity to the people of the region.

Planning
Currently there are very few lodges on the routes, but homestays are an option. For the time being these are relatively basic. Those who want more comforts and food other than dal bhat should plan on having a full service camping crew.

Itinerary and routes
There are basically two options for a trek here. A shorter choice is to trek from Sibang or Lumsung to Gurjakhani and return via Dhorpatan. Allow 5–6 days for this option. A 6–7 day add-on would then allow for an exploratory trek to the Churen Himal Base Camp. This option is described under the Hidden Villages Trek below.

A longer option is to start in Baglung and trek across the middle hills via Bonga Dhoban to Dhorpatan. From here there are two passes to Gurjakhani via Gurjaghat. This route allows a much more in-depth experience of the village life. This route is described under Gurja Himal Hidden Village Trek. Of course one can add Churen Himal to this option as well.

The following information is provided by Himalayan Map House; see map Gurja Himal & Hidden Village.

Gurja Himal Trek

Probably the most popular option in the Gurja Himal region, this trek combines the cultural gems of the area with the remote and little visited mountain grandeur of Churen Himal.

Gurja Himal Trek Summary	
Start	**Beni** (830m)
Finish	**Beni** (830m)
Distance	approx.70–80km (44–50 miles)
Time	8–10 days
Maximum altitude	**Rugachaur Pass** (4310m/14,140ft)
Trekking style	Homestay and camping
Transport	Bus, jeep and plane

Kathmandu – Pokhara

Take the flight or ease into the routines on the bus journey to Pokhara. Eat up; it's the last chance for a right royal banquet.

Pokhara – Darbang (9–10hrs)
Pokhara – Beni – Tatopani – Babiyachaur – Darbang

The trek begins with the exciting journey from Pokhara to Beni and Darbang (Darbanga). The road should be good when rebuilding has concluded to Beni, so that at least is a blessing. Those with more time can overnight in Beni. The jeep road onwards is not such a gift with rough and at times head-bumping sections. Following the Myagdi Khola valley the route climbs gently through Tatopani (985m) and Babiyachaur (970m) to the main roadhead at Darbang (1110m). It's generally quite a warm journey in these lower climes for much of the season, in stark contrast to what lies ahead. At the time of writing, the dirt road has been carved as far as Muna and is expected to reach Lumsung soon. Basic lodgings can be found in Darbang.

Darbang – Lulang (3 + 3–4hrs)
Darbang – Dharapani – Sibang – Muna – Lulang

The trekking today may be long or short depending on the state of the road from Darbang to Muna. The road climbs steadily along the Myagdi Khola valley through Dharapani, Takam, Sibang and Machhim to Muna. Where the trekking begins will depend on the road and transport. From Muna the trail/dirt track descends to cross the Dar Khola and climbs to **Lumsung** (2190m). There is a basic teahouse here. The way to Lulang is at the right fork of the junction. **Lulang** (2450m) is inhabited by the Bishwakarma people, who were the metal workers of the region. There is a homestay here run by Mina Mija (tel 974675748).

Mining methods

The Bishwakarma people were the main craftsmen of the region once the ore had been prised from the land. Their mining methods were very primitive and dangerous. Often only small cracks drenched in water gave access to the minerals. Tunnels were poorly ventilated and no form of shoring up of the mines was done. Light seems to have been provided by straw torches. Most of the ore was carried away by the village women. The ore was then ground into powder, with the denser particles allowed to sink, using water. The powder was then mixed with cow dung and heated in charcoal furnaces. The dung would burn away, allowing the fluid copper sulphate and oxides to coalesce and flow in channels to form ingots on cooling. These ingots were transported to Takam and sold on, often by Thakali traders who controlled the trade routes between India and Tibet along the Kali Gandaki.

Lulang – Gurjakhani (8–9hrs)
Lulang – Gurja Deurali – Gurjakhani

This is a long day, so an early start is essential. Once above the village, the trail climbs in rhododendron and oak forest. Beware of the mule caravans that supply the upper villages on the trail. It might take 3–4hrs to ascend to the Gurja Deurali pass (3250m), but the views from the top are worth all the effort. Due north is the massive wall of Gurja Himal (7193m). The trail descends in the forest to the canyon of the Dhaula Khola. It could take up to 4hrs to reach the river. After crossing the river, the path climbs for around 1hr to **Gurjakhani** (2620m).

Gurjakhani

The name Gurjakhani is derived from the mountain nearby and the word *khannu*, meaning to dig or mine. People first migrated to the region of the Dhaula valley 200–300 years ago. It was the search for minerals that began this movement. The Chantyal tribe came in search of the copper that was rumoured to exist in this general region. Chinese pilgrims reported the existence of trade between Nepal and Tibet of copper as well as lead, tin and iron. More recently, copper mining was greatly expanded during the Rana period from 1850–1950. After that time the mining industries in the area declined, as more convenient sources were found and different metals developed.

Today the village is a warren of alleys and lanes. The houses almost touch each other and many have intricately carved wooden windows. Around 250 houses now make up this predominantly farming community. Many people migrate to the lower valleys in winter. Homestay is the order of the day unless you are camping.

Various activities are on offer here, such as a visit to the mines, bird watching, observing the honey hunters, weaving and metal working, as well as pony trekking and cultural programs.

The Chantyal People

The Chantyal people, who number only about 10,000, live in the districts of Baglung and Myagdi. They are of Tibeto-Mongolian stock and have retained their unique language. The Chantyal were the first miners here. They were followed later by the Bishwakarma clans from the Kami caste, being the artisans who crafted the metals. Apparently the last miner died in 2014. Chantyal people are found in the Dhaulagiri Sanctuary area as well.

Gurja Himal viewpoint (2–3hrs)

About 1hr from the village is a spectacular viewpoint of Gurja Himal. The trail climbs from the school through an apple orchard to a corner where the view opens out.

Rhododendrons abound here and a return route descends via meadows and the sheepfold at Khegas.

Herding below Gurja Himal (Joy & Duane Poppe)

Gurjakhani – Gurjaghat (8–9hrs)
Gurjakhani – Rugachaur Pass – Gurjaghat

It's a tough day, but the views of the western peaks of Dhaulagiri from the Rugachaur pass are breathtaking. The approach from Gurjakhani to the pass is very steep. A local guide is vital for route-finding.

The trail heads west to cross the Dhaula Khola before climbing into the side tributary of the Huchin Khola. This route is often slippery and quite tiring, as the trail climbs along boulder-strewn gullies and above dense vegetation. The hour before the pass is extremely steep. The **Rugachaur pass** (3850m) has a fantastic panoramic view, though, to inspire. The whole range from Putha Himal to Dhaulagiri I grabs the attention. The trail down follows a broad valley that leads down to a more gently contouring path. Descending into the Simudar Khola valley, the route reaches **Gurjaghat** (3015m). Lodgings are available here.

Side trip: to Dhorpatan (2 days)

Eventually the road from Darbang is scheduled to be constructed all the way to Dhorpatan along the Uttar Ganga valley. Trekking this way will take a day each way at the moment. En route is the Bon monastery near Chhentung.

> **Chhentung Monastery**
> A Bon monastery in this part of the country is a rare sight, as most that remain are found in Dolpo, Mustang and close to the Tibetan border. A large retinue of Tibetan refugees were housed here after the 1960s. There is also a Tibetan Medical School in the area called Sowa Rigpa Medical Centre.

The Dhorpatan valley is quite a broad open area that has long attracted hunters who head for the reserve to the northwest. The valley is characterised by alpine meadows, coniferous glades, quiet rivers and a tranquil ambience. At Khalti Kutti one can find the Sunars community, who are renowned for their goldsmiths.

Gurjaghat – Lumsung (7–8hrs)
Gurjaghat – Jaljala Pass – Lumsung

The route heads east along the Uttar Ganga valley and in 3–4hrs climbs to the **Jaljala Pass** (3400m). Again the icy walls of the six peaks of Dhaulagiri are the star attraction. It takes a further 2–3hrs to reach the village of **Moreni** (2275m), with lodgings. Some may want to continue to Lumsung.

Lumsung – Darbang (3–4hrs + 2hrs)
Lumsung – Sibang – Dharapani – Darbang

However far the trekking continues from Lumsung, the inevitable dirt road will soon be encountered. The bumpy finale to **Darbang** is sure to be 'exciting'.

Darbang – Pokhara (9–10hrs)
Darbang – Babiyachaur – Tatopani – Beni – Pokhara

It's more of the same to Beni and then the 'tarmac' road takes over to Pokhara.

Churen Himal Base Camp

We have no detailed route information about this trek, so this itinerary is added from Himalayan Map House mapping sources and some local input from Mohan Chantyal in Gurjakhani. Be aware the information is not guaranteed to be accurate, and is merely here as a guideline. An experienced local guide is necessary, as well as a full camping crew. Try to get as much information as possible before contemplating this route. Regarding altitude gains, the approach to the base camp might be easier via the Lower West Dhaulagiri route that heads up the Keyarghe valley and over the ridge to Phalyaghar. From here the Kape Khola valley leads directly to Churen Himal Base Camp. For good planning and spare time, allow 6–7 days for this trek from Gurjakhani.

Gurjakhani – Jharchaur (5–6hrs)
Gurjakhani – Dalsing – Jharchaur

Following the newly designated Upper West Dhaulagiri Trail, the route climbs through **Dalsing** (2927m) along the northeast side of the Ketarghe Khola. With a high ridge ahead it's best to overnight in Jharchaur, which is quite a climb from Dalsing in any case.

Jharchaur – Bhujunge Camp (8–10hrs)
Jharchaur – Ridge – Bhujunge Camp

This looks like a demanding day, as the route climbs around and up along a ridge to the east. The altitude could easily make this difficult and very long, even though the distance is not great. An **intermediate camp** will probably be necessary, so add an extra day here when planning. Get local advice about the true altitude gains, as maps are not conclusive. After the **ridgeline**, camp is made at **Bhujunge Camp** (4284m).

Bhujunge Camp – Churen Base Camp (7–8hrs)
Bhujunge Camp – Churen Base Camp

The route descends to the **Kape Khola** valley, which might be a preferred if longer choice of approach to Churen Himal Base camp. This valley seems to have trails from the south via **Phalyaghar**, which look to be lower in altitude. The trail passes through **Dhungge Sanghu** but that's not saying there is any settlement there. Churen Himal Base Camp (4576m) sits directly below the summit of Churen Himal (7371m), so it must be a pretty stunning spot for a night or two.

Churen Himal B.C. – Jharchaur (8–9hrs)
Churen Himal BC – Bhujunge Camp – Jharchaur

Hopefully being now well acclimatised, the return trek should be a bit easier. It might still be wise to plan an extra day though, in case the trail is harder than predicted.

Jharchaur – Gurjakhani (4–5hrs)
Jharchaur – Dalsing – Gurjakhani

It's a bit quicker on the return stage, but maybe not so much. Arriving back in Gurjakhani might seem like coming home.

Gurja Himal Hidden Village Trek

The two trekking routes below can be combined to make a circular route of 9–10 days.

Baglung – Gurjakhani (6–7days)
Baglung – Phedi – Rum – Gurjaghat – Gurjakhani

This stage begins from the town of Baglung off the road from Pokhara to Beni. **Baglung** (970m) overlooks the Kali Gandaki and has a view of Dhaulagiri. The route is described on the back of the HMH Gurja Himal and Hidden Village map in some detail, so it will suffice here to outline the route and expected night stops only. The first stop en route is **Okhle**, (2310m), which is reached by utilising dirt roads and trails. Then it's over the **Kanchi Deurali** pass (2832m) to **Tarakholagaon** (1800m). Generally following the Tara Khola, the route comes to **Phedi** (2210m). A harder day follows across the ridges to **Rum** (1904m), and then it's on to **Bonga Doban (Dhobhan)** (1420m). Another long day follows over the **Gurjaghat Pass** (3350m) to **Gurjaghat** (3015m). An optional extra here allows a visit to **Dhorpatan**. The last day crosses the **Rugachaur Pass** (3850m) to **Gurjakhani** (2620m).

Milling in Gurja Himal (photo: Joy & Duane Poppe)

Gurjakhani – Darbang via Dhaula (3 days)
Gurjakhani – Lower Arche – Sibang – Darbang

Again the itinerary is set out on the above-mentioned map with overnight stages as follows. The first day is long (8hrs) from **Gurjakhani** (2620m) along the **Dhaula Canyon** to **Lower Arche** (1820m). Then the route is from Lower Arche to **Sibang** (1680m) across the Myagdi Khola valley. The last shorter day contours above the Myagdi valley via **Dharapani** and then on to **Darbang** (1070m). The dirt road has now reached Muna so the last stage to Darbang might be quicker. Jeeps ply the road to Beni and then Pokhara.

Side trip: Baglung – Tatopani (2 days)

Not its more famous cousin in the Kali Gandaki, this Tatopani is located north of Baglung in the Myagdi Khola valley. It's a short trip with an overnight at **Okhle** (2310m). From here the trail crosses the **Dhamja Pass** (2560m), which has one of the most outstanding panoramic views of Dhaulagiri. Road transport runs from Tatopani (890m) back to Beni.

Annapurna North Base Camp Trek

Introduction
Not strictly part of the Dhaulagiri region this future trek can be added to any crossing of the Ruwachaur Himal ridge from the Dhaulagiri Sanctuary.

Although the route was first used in 1950 by a French team led by Maurice Herzog, the route to the Annapurna North Base Camp is still a remote trek. In fact the French expedition was initially set on climbing Dhaulagiri and spent many weeks exploring above Jomsom. They even crossed the Thorong La to Manang before deciding that Annapurna I was the best target. Today the trail is rough, ill-defined in parts and very wild. Development is planned soon to make it a safe and usable trekking route.

Looking up the Mristi Khola and from various viewpoints further away, the trek will be a winner; high, wild, remote and enticing for its mountain grandeur. The following information has been collected from many sources and represents merely an expectation of what will be possible very soon. Hopefully all the current enthusiasm for opening the trail to recreational hikers will bear fruit and it will become an iconic trek.

Planning
Only the initial approaches have lodges, so this will still be for some time a fully supported camping trek. That means guides, cook and porters. It would be very wise to go equipped with crampons, ropes and ice axes if only for reassurance in the case of snowfall and bad weather. As far as we know, mountaineering experience will not be necessary on this route, but a head for heights and a willingness to forge these pioneering trails is advisable at this early stage of development. That said, the stage before the Thulobugin pass looks to be a challenge. Finding reliable water and flattish spaces to camp is still an issue.

At 4190m, it's not the highest base camp of any mountain in Nepal, so issues with altitude are less acute on this trek. However, there is an issue in the early stages of the trek.

Beginning the walk at Dana (1440m) is not ideal, because the highest point of the trek is before the base camp on the Thulobugin Pass (4310m). It would be better to start from Kalopani (2530m). Even then the trail climbs rapidly from Kalopani via Shepherd's Kharka (3260m) to the Thulobugin Pass (4310m). Ideally this requires a couple of intermediate camps on the ridge before crossing the pass, unless already acclimatised. For those with time, it will certainly not be out of the question to fly to Jomsom and explore the area around Muktinath before beginning this trek.

The usual factors concerning which season to try this route apply. Mid October to early December will offer the best clarity of views. Spring is the choice for those who hate the bitter cold and enjoy the flora.

No flights are required for access to the area unless heading for Jomsom and Muktinath to acclimatise. Otherwise it's buses or jeeps from Pokhara via Beni and Tatopani to Kalopani.

Itinerary and routes

The basic trek to Annapurna North Base Camp takes 15–16 days from Pokhara. If adding on an option from Jomsom to Muktinath allow at least 5–6 days extra.

From Pokhara buses and jeeps head via Beni and Tatopani to Kalopani. Once ensconced in one of the delightful lodges at Kalopani, there is time to study the imposing North Face of Annapurna I flanked by Fang (Barah Shikha or Bharha Chuli) – so many names but still a soaring spire at sunset. The trail departs along the Kali Gandaki River on the east side to Chhoya and climbs to Jhipra (Deurali). Shepherds Kharka is the first camp, already on the ridgeline. Thulobugin Pass is the main obstacle on the trek, and then it's mainly contouring around high above the Mristi Khola on above the tree line. How hard this route will prove is still largely a matter of conjecture. North Base Camp is located at the foot of the North Annapurna Glacier, surrounded by the regal giants of the Nilgiris, Tilicho, Khangsar Kang (Roc Noir) and Fang. It must be a stunning spot!

Various alternatives and side trips are likely to involve the route between Pokhara and Kalopani and from Dana back to Pokhara. Going via Ghorepani, with options via Tadapani and Ghandruk, or via Ulleri, are the main choices on offer. These are mentioned in the Dhaulagiri Kopra Panorama Trek section. See appendix for Itineraries and route suggestions.

Annapurna North Base Camp Trek Summary

Start	**Kalopani** (2530m)
Finish	**Tatopani** (1190m)
Distance	approx.50–55km (31–34 miles)
Time	15–16 days
Maximum altitude	**Thulobugin Pass** (4310m/14,140ft)
Trekking style	Lodges and camping
Transport	Bus, jeep and plane

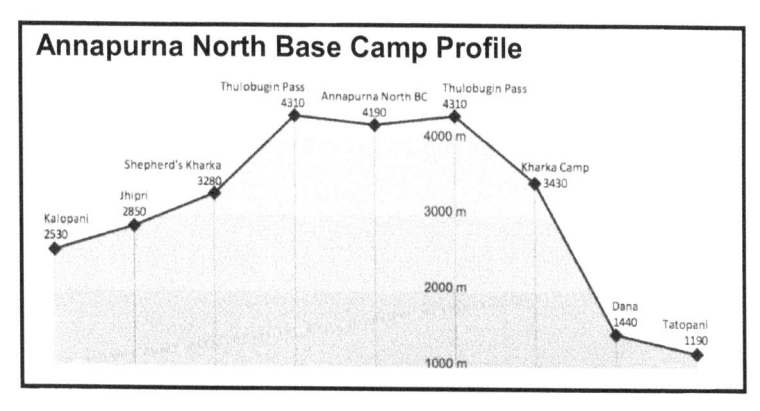

Annapurna North Base Camp Profile

Thulobugin Pass 4310
Annapurna North BC 4190
Thulobugin Pass 4310
Shepherd's Kharka 3280
Kharka Camp 3430
Jhipri 2850
Kalopani 2530
Dana 1440
Tatopani 1190

Annapurna I (on the left)

Boudhanath, a peaceful sanctuary in Kathmandu

> If you're young and fit
> Make the most of it.
> If you're old and slow,
> Mind how you go!
>
> Whatever you do
> Remember the rule:
> Don't mix attitude
> With altitude!

Cross those bridges when you get to them

Annapurna IV and II from Naudanda

The last word

Any trek in the highest mountains of the world will be laced with masses of eager anticipation and perhaps a little trepidation. The Himalaya were made for trekkers, hippies, pilgrims, philosophers, itinerants, climbers and adventurers. The reality far exceeds the dream. A trek in Nepal will rarely be a luxurious affair – with ghastly buses, brutal ascents, knee-grinding descents, midnight loo stops, hard beds, grungy dog patrols and relentless… exhausting… breathtaking… passes, but when all that privation is forgotten, the Himalaya become an incurable addiction.

> It's the beginning that's the worst, then the middle, then the end. But in the end, it's the end that's the worst.
> ***Samuel Beckett***

Have a safe and happy trek!

Things change – Boudhanath in 1975

APPENDICES

Appendix 1:
Trek summaries and suggested schedules

Grading
The degree of difficulty is defined in the following grades. The grades are relative but remember that there's hardly a flat area in Nepal.

Easy (A) – still requires effort with sections of steep ups and downs.

Moderate (B) is harder, including higher altitude.

Strenuous (C) involves steep climbs and exposed paths with some at altitude.

All treks listed require trekkers to be in good physical shape beforehand.

Note: Jeep or bus journeys are indicated as approximate. Elsewhere timings are split for jeep + trek time etc.

Climbing to Dhampus Pass (photo: Ade Summers)

Trekking routes	Time

Dhaulagiri Sanctuary Trek (B/C)

Day 1	Kathmandu – Pokhara	Flight or 6–8hrs
Day 2	Pokhara – Jhi	4+2hrs drive
Day 3	Jhi – Rayakhor	5–6hrs
Day 4	Rayakhor – Chhari	5–6hrs
Day 5	Chhari – Phedi	4–5hrs
Day 6	Phedi – Odar Camp	4–5hrs
Day 7	Odar Camp – South B.C.	3–5hrs
Day 8	Dhaulagiri Sanctuary	
Day 9	South B.C. – Duitakholsa	5–6hrs
Day 10	Duitakholsa – Chhari	6–7hrs
Day 11	Chhari – Chimkhola	4½–5½hrs
Day 12	Chimkhola – Dagnam	4–5hrs
Day 13	Dagnam – Pokhara	5–6hrs
Day 14	Pokhara – Kathmandu	Flight or 6–8hrs

Alternative:

Day 9	South B.C. – Odar	3–4hrs
Day 10	Odar – Phedi	3½–4hrs
Day 11	Phedi – Ghyasikharka	4½–5½hrs
Day 12	Ghyasikharka – Darmija	4–5hrs
Day 13	Darmija – Pokhara	2+2hrs
Day 14	Pokhara – Kathmandu	Flight or 6–8hrs

Dhaulagiri Sanctuary: One Week

Day 1	Pokhara – Jhi	4+2hrs drive
Day 2	Jhi – Rayakhor	5–6hrs
Day 3	Rayakhor – Chhari	5–6hrs
Day 4	Chhari – Phedi	4–5hrs
Day 5	Phedi – Ghyasikharka	4½–5½hrs
Day 6	Ghyasikharka – Darmija	4–5hrs
Day 7	Darmija – Pokhara	2+2hrs

Trekking routes   Time

Dhaulagiri Sanctuary Plus Trek (B/C+)

Day 1	Kathmandu – Pokhara	Flight or 6–8hrs
Day 2	Pokhara – Jhi	4+2hrs drive
Day 3	Jhi – Rayakhor	5–6hrs
Day 4	Rayakhor – Chhari	5–6hrs
Day 5	Chhari – Phedi	4–5hrs
Day 6	Phedi – Odar Camp	4–5hrs
Day 7	Odar Camp – South B.C.	3–5hrs
Day 8	Dhaulagiri Sanctuary	
Day 9	South B.C. – Phedi	7–8hrs
Day 10	Phedi – Pairo Kharka	6–8hrs
Day 11	Pairo Kharka – Forest Camp	7–9hrs
Day 12	Forest Camp – Lete	7–9hrs
Day 13	Lete – Dana	7–8hrs
Day 14	Dana – Tatopani	2–3hrs
Day 15	Tatopani – Pokhara	5–7hrs drive
Day 16	Pokhara – Kathmandu	6–8hrs bus

Alternative: 1

Day 13	Lete – Dana	3–4hrs drive
Day 14	Dana – Shikha	3–4hrs drive?
Day 15	Shikha – Ghorepani	5–6hrs
Day 16	Ghorepani – Tadapani	5–6hrs
Day 17	Tadapani – Ghandruk	3–4hrs
Day 18	Ghandruk – Pokhara	4–6hrs
Day 19	Pokhara – Kathmandu	6–8hrs bus

Alternative: 2

Day 13	Lete – Dana	3–4hrs drive
Day 14	Dana – Shikha	3–4hrs drive
Day 15	Shikha – Ghorepani	5–6hrs
Day 16	Ghorepani – Tirkhedunga	5–6hrs
Day 17	Tirkhedunga – Pokhara	5–6hrs
Day 18	Pokhara – Kathmandu	6–8hrs bus

Trekking routes   Time

Dhaulagiri Circuit Trek (C/C+)

Day 1	Kathmandu – Pokhara	Flight or 6–8hrs bus
Day 2	Pokhara–Babiyachaur/Darbang	6–10hrs drive
Day 3	Babiyachaur – Dharapani	6–7hrs
Day 4	Dharapani – Muri	5–6hrs
Day 5	Muri – Boghara	6–7hrs
Day 6	Boghara – Dobang	6–7hrs
Day 7	Dobang – Sallaghari	5–6hrs
Day 8	Sallaghari – Italian Camp	3–4hrs
Day 9	Italian Camp	
Day 10	Italian Camp – Glacier Camp	5–6hrs
Day 11	Glacier Camp	
Day 12	Glacier Camp – Dhaulagiri B.C.	5–6hrs
Day 13	Dhaulagiri Base Camp	
Day 14	Dhaulagiri B.C. – Hidden Valley	7–8hrs
Day 15	Dhampus Peak option	
Day 16	Hidden Valley – Yak Kharka	8–9hrs
Day 17	Yak Kharka – Alu Bari	2–3hrs
Day 18	Alu Bari – Marpha/Jomsom	4–5hrs +1hr drive
Day 19	Jomsom – Pokhara	30mins flight
Day 20	Pokhara/spare	
Day 21	Pokhara – Kathmandu	Flight or 6–8hrs bus

Trekking routes   Time

Dhaulagiri Circuit Trek (C/C+)

Alternative: If the dirt road is open to Muna

Day 1	Kathmandu – Pokhara	Flight or 6–8hrs bus
Day 2	Pokhara – Darbang	9–10hrs drive
Day 3	Darbang – Phaliyagaon	3–4hrs drive
Day 4	Phaliyagaon – Muri	2–3hrs
Day 5	Muri – Boghara	6–7hrs
Day 6	Boghara – Dobang	6–7hrs
Day 7	Dobang – Sallaghari	5–6hrs
Day 8	Sallaghari – Italian Camp	3–4hrs
Day 9	Italian Camp	
Day 10	Italian Camp – Glacier Camp	5–6hrs
Day 11	Glacier Camp	
Day 12	Glacier Camp – Dhaulagiri B.C.	5–6hrs
Day 13	Dhaulagiri Base Camp	
Day 14	Dhaulagiri B.C. – Hidden Valley	7–8hrs
Day 15	Hidden Valley – Yak Kharka	8–11hrs
Day 16	Yak Kharka – Marpha/Jomsom	4–7hrs +1hrs drive
Day 17	Jomsom – Pokhara	9–10hrs drive
Day 18	Pokhara/spare	
Day 19	Pokhara – Kathmandu	Flight or 6–8hrs bus

Trekking routes

Dhaulagiri Dolpo Trek (B/C+)

Day	Route	Time
Day 1	Kathmandu – Pokhara	6–8hrs bus
Day 2	Pokhara – Beni	3–5hrs jeep or bus
Day 3	Beni – Darbang	5–7hrs jeep
Day 4	Darbang – Muna	3–4hrs
Day 5	Muna – Moreni	3–4hrs
Day 6	Moreni – Gurjaghat	8–9hrs
Day 7	Gurjaghat – Chhentung	3–4hrs
Day 8	Chhentung – Dhorpatan	2–3hrs
Day 9	Dhorpatan – Thankur	5–6hrs
Day 10	Thankur – Pelma	5–7hrs
Day 11	Pelma – Maikot	5–6hrs
Day 12	Maikot – Sen Khola	4–5hrs
Day 13	Sen Khola – Jang La Phedi	5–6hrs
Day 14	Jang La Phedi – Tarakot	6–8hrs
Day 15	Tarakot – Laina Odar	4–5hrs
Day 16	Laina Odar – Toltol	7–9hrs
Day 17	Toltol – Dho Tarap	6–8hrs
Day 18	Dho Tarap – Upper Panzang	6–8hrs
Day 19	Upper Panzang – Chharka	5–7hrs
Day 20	Chharka – Nulungsumda	8–10hrs
Day 21	Nulungsumda – Galden	6–8hrs
Day 22	Galden – Santa	4–5hrs
Day 23	Santa – Kagbeni	8–9hrs
Day 24	Kagbeni – Jomsom	3hrs
Day 25	Jomsom – Pokhara	Flight or 12hrs +
Day 26	Pokhara – Kathmandu	Flight or 6–8hrs bus
Day 27	Spare	

Trekking routes Time
Dhaulagiri Dolpo Trek (C/C+)
Alternative: via Mukut
Timings in the Mukut area are estimated

Day 1	Kathmandu – Pokhara	6–8hrs bus
Day 2	Pokhara – Beni	3–5hrs jeep or bus
Day 3	Beni – Darbang	5–7hrs jeep
Day 4	Darbang – Muna	3–4hrs
Day 5	Muna – Moreni	3–4hrs
Day 6	Moreni – Gurjaghat	8–9hrs
Day 7	Gurjaghat – Chhentung	3–4hrs
Day 8	Chhentung – Dhorpatan	2–3hrs
Day 9	Dhorpatan – Thankur	5–6hrs
Day 10	Thankur – Pelma	5–7hrs
Day 11	Pelma – Maikot	5–6hrs
Day 12	Maikot – Sen Khola	4–5hrs
Day 13	Sen Khola – Jang La Phedi	5–6hrs
Day 14	Jang La Phedi – Tarakot	6–7hrs
Day 15	Tarakot – Laisicap	4–5hrs
Day 16	Laisicap – Kakkotgaon	5–6hrs
Day 17	Kakkotgaon – Gharengaon	5–6hrs
Day 18	Gharengaon – Mukut	3–4hrs
Day 19	Mukut	
Day 20	Mukut – High Camp	6–9hrs
Day 21	High Camp – Nulungsumda	5–7hrs
Day 22	Nulungsumda – Galden	6–8hrs
Day 23	Galden – Santa	4–5hrs
Day 24	Santa – Kagbeni	8–9hrs
Day 25	Kagbeni – Jomsom	3hrs
Day 26	Jomsom – Pokhara	Flight
Day 27	Pokhara – Kathmandu	Flight or 6–8hrs bus
Day 28	Spare	

Trekking routes   **Time**

Dhaulagiri Kopra Panorama Trek (B/C)

Day 1	Kathmandu – Pokhara	Flight or 6–8hrs bus
Day 2	Pokhara – Landruk	6½–7½hrs
Day 3	Landruk – Tadapani	6–7hrs
Day 4	Tadapani – Dobaato	5–6hrs
Day 5	Dobaato – Chistibung	3–4hrs
Day 6	Chistibung – Kopra Ridge	3–4hrs
Day 7	Kopra Ridge – en route Camp	4hrs
Day 8	Camp – Khairetal – Kopra	
Day 9	Kopra Ridge – Chitre	4–5hrs
Day 10	Chitre – Ghorepani	2hrs
Day 11	Ghorepani – Tirkhedunga	4–5hrs
Day 12	Tirkhedunga – Pokhara	3–4hrs+2hrs drive
Day 13	Pokhara – Kathmandu	Flight or 6–8hrs bus

Parbat Myagdi Link Trek (B)

Day 1	Phalante – Mohare Danda	6–7hrs
Day 2	Mohare Danda – Nangi	3–4hrs
Day 3	Nangi – Danda Khetri	2–3hrs
Day 4	Danda Khetri – Banskhara	2hrs
Day 5	Banskhara – Galeshwar	1–2hrs

Parbat Myagdi Circular Trek (B)

Day 1	Pokhara – Galeshwar	4–5hrs drive
Day 2	Galeshwar– Banskhara	2hrs
Day 3	Banskhara – Danda Khetri	2–3hrs
Day 4	Danda Khetri – Nangi	2–3hrs
Day 5	Nangi – Mohare Danda	4–5hrs
Day 6	Mohare Danda – Tikot	6–7hrs
Day 7	Tikot – Tiplyang	2–3hrs
Day 8	Tiplyang – Pokhara	

Trekking routes Time

Gurja Himal Trek (B/C)

Day 1	Kathmandu – Pokhara	Flight or 6–8hrs bus
Day 2	Pokhara – Darbang	9–10hrs drive
Day 3	Darbang – Lulang	3+3–4hrs
Day 4	Lulang – Gurjakhani	8–9hrs
Day 5	Gurjakhani – Gurjaghat	8–9hrs
Day 6	Gurjaghat – Dhorpatan	5–6hrs optional
Day 7	Dhorpatan – Gurjaghat	5–6hrs
Day 8	Gurjaghat – Lumsung	7–8hrs
Day 9	Lumsung – Darbang	3–4hrs+2
Day 10	Darbang – Beni	5–6hrs drive
Day 11	Beni – Pokhara	3–4hrs drive
Day 12	Pokhara – Kathmandu	Flight or 6–8hrs bus

Churen Himal Base Camp (B/C+)

Itinerary and timings estimated only

Day 1	Gurjakhani – Jharchaur	5–6hrs
Day 2	Jharchaur – Bhujunge Camp	8–10hrs
Day 3	Bhujunge Camp – Churen BC	7–8hrs
Day 4	Base Camp	
Day 5	Churen BC – Jharchaur	8–9hrs
Day 6	Jharchaur – Gurjakhani	4–5hrs

Gurja Himal & Hidden Village (B/C)

Day 1	Kathmandu – Pokhara	Flight or 6–8hrs bus
Day 2	Pokhara – Baglung	3–4hrs drive
Day 3	Baglung – Okhle	6–7hrs
Day 4	Okhle – Phedi	6–7hrs
Day 5	Phedi – Rum	5–6hrs
Day 6	Rum – Bonga Dhoban	8–9hrs
Day 7	Bonga Dhoban – Gurjaghat	8–9hrs
Day 8	Gurjaghat – Gurjakhani	8–9hrs
Day 9	Gurjakhani – Lower Arche	7–8hrs
Day 10	Lower Arche – Sibang	5–6hrs
Day 11	Sibang – Darbang	4–5hrs
Day 12	Darbang – Beni	5–6hrs drive
Day 13	Beni – Pokhara	3–4hrs drive
Day 14	Pokhara – Kathmandu	Flight or 6–8hrs bus

Trekking routes Time

Annapurna North Base Camp Trek (C)

This sample itinerary is included for future information. Daily stops and timings are estimated only.

Day 1	Kathmandu – Pokhara	Flight or 6–8hrs bus
Day 2	Pokhara – Kalopani	7–9hrs
Day 3	Kalopani – Chhoya	1–2hrs
Day 4	Chhoya – Shepherd Kharka	6–7hrs
Day 5	Shepherd Kharka – High Camp	6–7hrs
Day 6	High Camp – Higher Camp	5–6hrs
Day 7	Higher Camp – North B.C.	6–7hrs
Day 8	North Base Camp	
Day 9	North B.C. – Higher Camp	5–6hrs
Day 10	Higher Camp – Ridge Camp	5–6hrs
Day 11	Ridge Camp – Kharka	6–7hrs
Day 12	Kharka – Dana	5–6hrs
Day 13	Dana – Beni	2–4hrs
Day 14	Beni – Pokhara	3–4hrs
Day 15	Pokhara – Kathmandu	35mins flight
Day 16	Spare	

Appendix 2: Bibliography

Allen, Charles **A Mountain in Tibet** 1982
Allen, Charles **The Search for Shangrila** Little, Brown and Company, London 1999
Anderson, Mary. **Festivals of Nepal** George Allen & Unwin 1971
Batchelor, Stephen **The Tibet Guide** Wisdom Publications Inc., USA, 1998
Bell, Charles **The People of Tibet** Clarendon Press 1928 reprinted by Book Faith India 1998
Bista, Dor Bahadur. **People of Nepal** Ratna Pustak Bhandar 1987
Boustead, Robin. **Nepal Trekking and the Great Himalaya Trail** Trailblazer 2011
Bowman, W E (Bill). **The Ascent of Rum Doodle** 1956 (www.rumdoodle.org.uk – a great skit on the big mountaineering expeditions of the past, written long before they became in vogue)
Chorlton, Windsor and Wheeler, Nik. **Cloud-Dwellers of the Himalayas** Time-Life Books 1982
Chan, Victor **Tibet Handbook** Moon Publications 1994
Dalai Lama. **An Introduction to Buddhism and Tantric Meditation** Paljor Publications 1996
Durkan, David. **Penguins on Everest** Swami Kailash 2012, 2014, 2016
Fleming. **Birds of Nepal** reprints by Indian publishers
Dorje, Gyurme **Tibet** Footprint Handbooks 2004
Francke, Rev. A. H. **A History of Western Tibet** 1907 reprinted by Pilgrims 1998
Gibbons, Bob & Pritchard-Jones, Siân. **Kathmandu: Valley of the Green-Eyed Yellow Idol** Pilgrims 2004
Gibbons, Bob & Pritchard-Jones, Siân. **Annapurna: A Trekkers' Guide** Cicerone 2013, 2017
Gibbons, Bob & Pritchard-Jones, Siân. **Mount Kailash: A Trekkers' Guide** Cicerone 2007
Gordon, Antoinette. **The Iconography of Tibetan Lamaism** Munshi Ram M Delhi 1978
Govinda, Lama Anagarika. **The Way of the White Clouds** Rider and Company, London 1966

Hagen, Toni. **Nepal: The Kingdom of the Himalayas** Kümmerley and Frey 1980
Handa, O. C. **Buddhist Western Himalaya** Indus Publishing, New Delhi 2001
Handa, O. C. **Buddhist Monasteries of Himalchal** Indus Publishing, New Delhi 2004
Hedin, Sven **A Conquest of Tibet** Book Faith India reprinted 1994
Kalsang, Ladrang. **The Guardian Deities of Tibet** Winsome Books India 2003
Lama, Sonam and Lama, Lopsang Chhiring **Manaslu and Tsum Valley** Himalayan Map House
Landon, Perceval. **Nepal Vols I and II** Pilgrims 200
Lhalungpa, Lobsang P. **The Life of Milarepa** BFI 1997
Lonely Planet **Nepali Phrasebook** Frequently published
Mierow, Dorothy and Shrestha, Tirtha Bahadur. **Himalayan Flowers and Trees** Prakashan/Pilgrims
Noyce, Wilfred. **Climbing the Fish's Tail'** Heinemann, 1958, reprinted by Book Faith/Pilgrims Publishing, 1998
O'Connor, Bill. **Adventure Treks: Nepal** Crowood 1990
Pauler, Gerda. **The Great Himalaya Trail** Baton Wick 2013
Pritchard-Jones, Siân & Gibbons, Bob. **Himalayan Travel Guides: Manaslu, Dolpo, Ganesh Himal & Tamang Heritage Trail, Langtang, Everest, Rolwaling, Mustang, Kanchenjunga, Makalu, West Nepal, Dhaulagiri, Nepal Himalaya** Himalayan Map House and CreateSpace 2013–18
Pritchard-Jones, Siân and Gibbons, Bob. **Kailash and Guge: Land of the Tantric Mountain** Pilgrims 2006
Pritchard-Jones, Siân and Gibbons, Bob. **Ladakh: Land of Magical Monasteries** Pilgrims 2006
Pritchard-Jones, Siân and Gibbons, Bob. **Earthquake Diaries: Nepal 2015** Expedition World 2015
Pritchard-Jones, Siân and Gibbons, Bob. **In Search of the Green-Eyed Yellow Idol** Expedition World 2015
Pye-Smith, Charlie. **Travels in Nepal** Aurum Press 1988
Reynolds, Kev. **Trekking in the Himalaya** Cicerone 2013
Reynolds, Kev. **Abode of the Gods** Cicerone 2015
Roerich, Nicholas. **Altai Himalaya** 1929, reprinted by Book Faith India 1996
Snellgrove, David. **Buddhist Himalaya** Oxford 1957
Snellgrove, David **Himalayan Pilgrimage** Oxford 1961

Tilman, H W. **Nepal Himalaya** Cambridge University Press /Diadem Books–The Mountaineers 1983
Tucci, Giuseppe. **Shrines of a Thousand Buddhas** reprinted Pilgrims, Varanasi 2008

Films
A wonderfully evocative film about the people of Dolpo in Nepal, **Himalaya** (first released as **Caravan** in Nepal) portrays the life of traditional village yak herders in the remote regions. Not about Nepal but good background is **Seven Years in Tibet**, about Heinrich Harrer's life as a fugitive from World War II and his life in Lhasa close to the Dalai Lama. A more recent release is **Himalaya Bhotia**, a French-made film about the people of northern Nepal, such as Tamang, Dolpa, Sherpa and others.

Music
There are a lot of new CDs on Himalayan themes. A few are folk songs, others are amalgams of Tibetan chants, songs and 'Western Oriental'. These tunes resonate with calming and meditative music. Some are **Tibetiya, Sacred Buddha, Karmapa: Secrets of the Crystal Mountain, Journey to Tibet, Sacred Chants of Buddha**, sound track of the film **Himalaya, Nepali Folksongs**. All these can be found in Kathmandu for Rs200–500.

Trailside shrine (photo: Sanjib Gurung)

Appendix 3: Glossary

Religious and other terminology

Significant Buddhist deities

The **Dhyani Buddhas** face the four cardinal directions; they are often found on stupas and chaityas (small stone chortens). The Dhyani Buddhas were created from the wisdom of the Adi (first) Buddha, the primordial Buddha. **Vairocana** is the first Dhyani Buddha and resides in the stupa sanctum; Vairocana is the illuminator, to light the way. **Akshobhya** faces east; **Amitabha** faces west; **Amoghasiddhi** faces north, with a seven-headed serpent behind him; **Ratna Sambhava** faces south (these are the Sanskrit names).

The following are some other important deities; Sanskrit names are shown first.

Sakyamuni (Sakya Tukpa) The mortal Buddha, Gautama Siddhartha, born in Nepal.
Avalokiteshvara (Chenresig) Bodhisattva having renounced Nirvana, the end of the cycle of rebirth. He embodies compassion (*karuna*) and remains on earth to counter suffering. The Dalai Lama is considered to be his earthly representative.
Amitayus (Tsepame) Buddha of Boundless Life, an aspect of Amitabha; he is associated with longevity.
Vajrapani (Channa Dorje) Spiritual son of Akshobhya. He carries a *dorje* (*vajra*) and is a powerful, wrathful protector. He has monstrous Tantric powers and wears a snake around his neck.
Hayagriva (Tamdrin) Wrathful emanation of Chenresig, guards many shrines. Blood red with a small horse sticking out of his head, he wears a garland of skulls.
Manjushri (Jampelyang) God of wisdom, who carries a sword to cut through ignorance. Worshipping Manjushri gives intellect and intelligence.
Yamantaka (Dorje Jigje) 'Slayer of death', a wrathful emanation of Manjushri; a Gelug-pa deity with a buffalo head.

Tara (Drolma) Sacred to both Buddhists and Hindus, representing the maternal aspect, symbolising fertility, purity and compassion. With 21 versions, Tara appears in different colours: red, green, white and gold, and as Kali, dark blue, representing different aspects of her nature.
Maitreya Buddha (Jampa/Champa) The future Buddha.
Medicine Buddha Engaged for healing the sick, often a blue colour with four hands.
Mahakala Linked to Shiva with his trident. He tramples on corpses and is a wrathful Avalokiteshvara.
The Four Harmonious Friends
Found in many monasteries, depicting four animals, one on top of the other: the Elephant, Monkey, Rabbit and Bird. These represent harmony, peace and the removal of conflict.
The Four Guardians Seen at monastery entrances. Dhitarashtra is the white guardian of the east, holding a flute. Virupaksha guards the west; he is red with a stupa in one hand and a serpent in the other. Virudhakla is guardian of the south, holding a blue sword. Vaisravana guards the north, holding a yellow banner and a mongoose, usually seen vomiting jewels.
Padma Sambhava (Guru Rinpoche) The most famous icon of Buddhism, an Indian Tantric master who went to Tibet in the eighth century. He established the Nyingma-pa Red Hat sect. His consort Yeshe Tsogyal recorded his teachings to be revealed to future generations.
Milarepa Tibet's poet, magician and saint – a historical figure, associated with many legends. He meditated in caves as a hermit before achieving realisation.

Significant Bon deities

Bon has four main peaceful deities, the 'Four Transcendent Lords': Shenlha Wokar, Satrig Ersang, Sangpo Bumtri and Tonpa Shenrap Miwoche.
Others include: **Kuntu Zangpo** (similar to the primordial Adi Buddha of Buddhism); **Kunzang Gyalwa Gyatso** (very similar, and perhaps a precursor to the 1000-armed Avalokiteshvara); **Welse Ngampa** (a nine-headed protector representing 'piercing ferocity' and crushing the enemies of Bon); **Sipai Gyalmo** (a protectress called the 'Queen of the World').

Other definitions

Arhat Original disciples of Buddha who have managed to become free from the cycle of existence (samsara). Arhats are not often seen as icons, but when they are, their faces have moustaches and beards.
Bharal Species of blue sheep.
Bhatti Small rural dwelling.
Bodhisattva Disciple of Buddha who has delayed the attainment of Nirvana in order to teach.
Bon Pre-Buddhist religion of Tibet.
Chang Home-brewed barley wine/beer, sometimes made with other grain.
Chorten Similar to a small stupa (see below) but does not normally contain relics.
Dakini Female deity who can fly.
Dorje/Vajra Thunderbolt: it destroys ignorance. A complex figure-of-eight-shaped metal object found at many temples and shrines.
Dzong Fortress, castle.
Gompa Tibetan word for a monastery or holy place.
Gonkhang Small, dark and somewhat forbidding chamber housing the protecting deities: Yamantaka, Mahakala and Palden Lhamo, among others.
Kani Entrance archway to settlements.
Kharka Herders' shelter and meadow.
Kora Circular pilgrimage trek around a sacred mountain or lake.
Lama Religious teacher and guide, male or female.
Lhakhang Temple chapel within a monastery.
Losar Tibetan New Year festival.
Mandala Circular pattern made of many colours, often a square or squares within a circle. Represents 'the divine abode of an enlightened being.
Mani stone Rock covered with engraved Buddhist mantras, sometimes painted.
Mani wall Long wall made of flat stones engraved with Buddhist mantras; may also contain prayer wheels. You should always keep these on your right.
Palden Lhamo Fearful Tibetan female goddess, always on horseback.

Paubha Religious painting on cloth, specific to the Kathmandu Valley. Predates the Tibetan thangka.

Prayer flag Seen in five colours, on which prayers are printed; these flutter in the wind, sending prayers direct to heaven. The colours represent the five elements: earth, fire, air, water, and ether.

Prayer wheel Engraved cylinder with Tibetan script and containing prayers. Generally fixed into a wall, or hand held and spun while walking; the spinning action activates the prayers.

Puja Ceremony offering prayers.

Rakshi Nepalese alcoholic drink, not always healthily prepared.

Rigsum Gonpo Three chortens seen above kanis and elsewhere, representing the three deities who offer protection to villages. The red chorten represents Manjushri, giving wisdom; the white chorten represents Avalokiteshvara, offering compassion; and the blue, black or grey chorten represents Vajrapani, to fight off evil. They ward off many spirits found in the three worlds: sky, earth and underworld.

Sadhu Self-proclaimed holy man/ascetic.

Sago Namgo Seen in the northern regions, these strange objects give protection against bad omens. They relate to the 'Mother Earth spirits' and translate as Earth Door and Sky Door. Made from ram skulls, wood or fabric.

Sky burial Form of burial where the body is cut up and fed to the vultures and large birds.

Stupa Large monument, usually with a square base, a dome and a pointed spire on top. The spire represents the levels towards enlightenment. A stupa may often host the remains of a revered lama or teacher.

Tantra Oral teachings and Buddhist scriptures, describing the use of mantras, mandalas and deities in meditation and yoga. It is commonly associated with physical methods of striving for enlightenment but equally applicable to meditation methods using the energies of the mind.

Thangka/tangka Religious painting, usually on silk fabric. They are often seen in all monasteries, hanging on walls or pillars.

Tsampa Traditional Tibetan food: roasted barley mixed with butter tea, it is made into a sort of porridge.

Vajrayana Buddhism 'Diamond' branch of the religion found in Tibet and associated with Tantric ideas.
Yab-yum Depiction of two deities, male and female. The male represents compassion and the female wisdom. Deities depict the spiritual union and higher awareness.
Yidam A personal tutelary deity used in meditation practice.

Monastery images

Appendix 4: Nepali language hints

> Language is an impotent substitute for experience.
> *Abode of the Gods*, **Kev Reynolds**

Useful words and phrases

Hello/Goodbye	*Namaste*
Goodnight	*Suva ratri*
How are you?	*Tapailai kasto chha?*
Very well	*Ramro chha*
Thank you	*Dhanyabad*
Yes (it is)	*Ho*
No (it isn't)	*Hoina*
Yes (have)	*Chha*
No (don't have)	*Chhaina*
OK	*Tik chha*
What is your name?	*Tapaiko naam ke ho?*
My name is Sanjib	*Mero naam Sanjib ho*
Please go slowly	*Bistaari jaane*
Where is a lodge?	*Lodge kahaa chha?*
What's the name of this village?	*Yo gaaunko naam ke ho?*
Which trail goes to Phedi?	*Phedi jaane baato kun ho?*
Where are you going?	*Tapaai kahaa jaane?*
I don't understand	*Maile buhjina*
I don't know	*Ta chhaina*
Please give me a cup of tea	*Chiyaa dinos*
How much is it?	*Kati paisa*
Where is the toilet?	*Chaarpi kahaa chha?*
Where is there water?	*Pani kahaa chha?*
I want to rent a pony	*Malaai ghoda bhadama chaainchha*
I need a porter	*Ma kulli chaainchha*
I am sick	*Ma biraami chhu*
I have altitude sickness	*Lekh laagyo*

Other useful words

what	*ke*
where	*kun*
when	*kaile*
how much	*kati*

good	*ramro*
bad	*naramro*
cold	*jaaro/chiso*
hot	*garam/tato*
trail	*baato*
steeply up	*ukaalo*
steeply down	*oraalo*
flat	*terso*
dangerous	*aptero*
river (small)	*khola*
stream	*kholsa*

Food

food	*khanaa*
spinach	*sag*
bread	*roti*
rice	*bhat*
noodle soup	*thukpa*
eggs	*phul*
meat	*maasu*
yoghurt	*dahi*
sugar	*chini*
salt	*nun*
water	*pani*
boiled water	*umaalekho pani*
black tea	*kalo chiyaa*
hot water	*tatopani*
cold water	*chiso pani*

Numbers

1	*ek*	11	*ekhaara*
2	*dui*	12	*baara*
3	*tin*	15	*pandhra*
4	*char*	20	*bis*
5	*paanch*	30	*tis*
6	*chha*	40	*chaalis*
7	*saat*	50	*pachaas*
8	*aath*	100	*ek say*
9	*nau*	500	*panch say*
10	*das*	1000	*ek hajaar*

Appendix 5: Useful contacts

Tour operators in Nepal

Advent Himalaya www.adventhimalayatreks.com
Alliance Treks www.rubyvalleytreks.com
Ama Dablam Adventures www.adventure-himalaya.com
Asian Trekking www.asian-trekking.com
Beyond the Limits www.treksinnepal.com
Bochi Bochi www.bochi-bochitrek.com
Climbing Himalaya www.climbinghimalaya.com
Dream Himalaya www.dreamhimalaya.com.np
Explore Dolpo www.exploredolpotrekking.com
Firante Treks www.firante.com
Friends Adventure Team www.friendsadventure.com
Himalayan Deep Breath Trek www.hdbtrek.com
Himalayan Encounters www.himalayanencounters.com
Himalayan Glacier Trekking www.himalayanglacier.com
Himalayan Rock www.himalayanrock.com
Nepal Nature dot com www.nepalnaturetravels.com
Off the Wall www.offthewalltrekking.com
Responsible Treks www.responsibletreks.com
Sacred Himalaya www.sacredhimalaya.com
Sanjib Gurung www.climbinghimalaya.com
Sherpa Adventure Travel www.sherpaadventure.com
3 Sisters Adventure www.3sistersadventure.com
Trinetra Adventure www.trinetra-adventure.com
Trip Himalaya www.triphimalaya.com

The authors have either worked with these providers or know them from experience; many more can be found online.

Tour operators overseas

Classic Journeys www.classicjourneys.co.uk
Exodus www.exodus.co.uk
Expedition World www.expeditionworld.com (travel site run by the authors)

Explore www.explore.co.uk
Intrepid Travel www.intrepidtravel.com
Kamzang Journeys www.kamzang.com
KE Adventure Travel www.keadventure.com
Mountain Kingdoms www.mountainkingdoms.com
Paulo Grobel www.paulogrobel.com
Peregrine www.peregrineadventures.co.uk
Sherpa Expeditions www.sherpa-walking-holidays.co.uk
Take On Nepal (Batase Trails) www.takeonnepal.com.au
The Adventure Company www.adventurecompany.co.uk
The Mountain Company www.themountaincompany.co.uk
Trekking Team Poland www.trampingi.pl
Wilderness Travels USA www.wildernesstravels.com
World Expeditions www.worldexpeditions.co.uk

Online information
www.gov.uk/foreign-travel-advice – travel advice and tips
www.himalayanrescue.org – rescue information
www.info-nepal.com – general background
www.nepalimmigration.gov.np – immigration department for visas and permits
www.kmtnc.org.np – conservation themes
www.mnteverest.net/trek.html – list of trekking companies
www.nepalmountaineering.org
www.taan.org.np – Trekking Agencies Association of Nepal
www.visitnepal.com – travel information
www.welcomenepal.com – tourist information
www.ekantipur.com – news
www.nepalnews.net – news
www.nepalnow.com – news
www.stanfords.co.uk – maps
www.themapshop.co.uk – maps
www.trekkingpartners.com – to find a trekking partner
www.trekmag.com – French magazine

Important phone numbers
Fire Brigade 101
Police Control 100
Telephone Inquiries 197
Tribhuvan International Airport 4471933

Hospitals
B & B Hospital 5533206
Bir Hospital 4222862/63
Kanti Children's Hospital 4427452
Norvic Hospital 4258554
Patan Hospital 5522266
TU Teaching Hospital 4412505

Police
District Police Office, Kathmandu 4261945
District Police Office, Lalitpur 5521207
Emergency Police Service 4226999

Embassies
Australia, Bansbari 4371678
British, Lainchour 4411590
China, Baluwatar 4411740
France, Lazimpat 4418034
India, Lainchour 4414990
Japan, Panipokhari 4426680
Thailand, Bansbari 4371410
USA, Maharajgunj 4411179

Please note that all phone numbers are likely to change.

Mysterious glade on the trail

Dhaulagiri from the trail to Mulpani

Map of Nepal

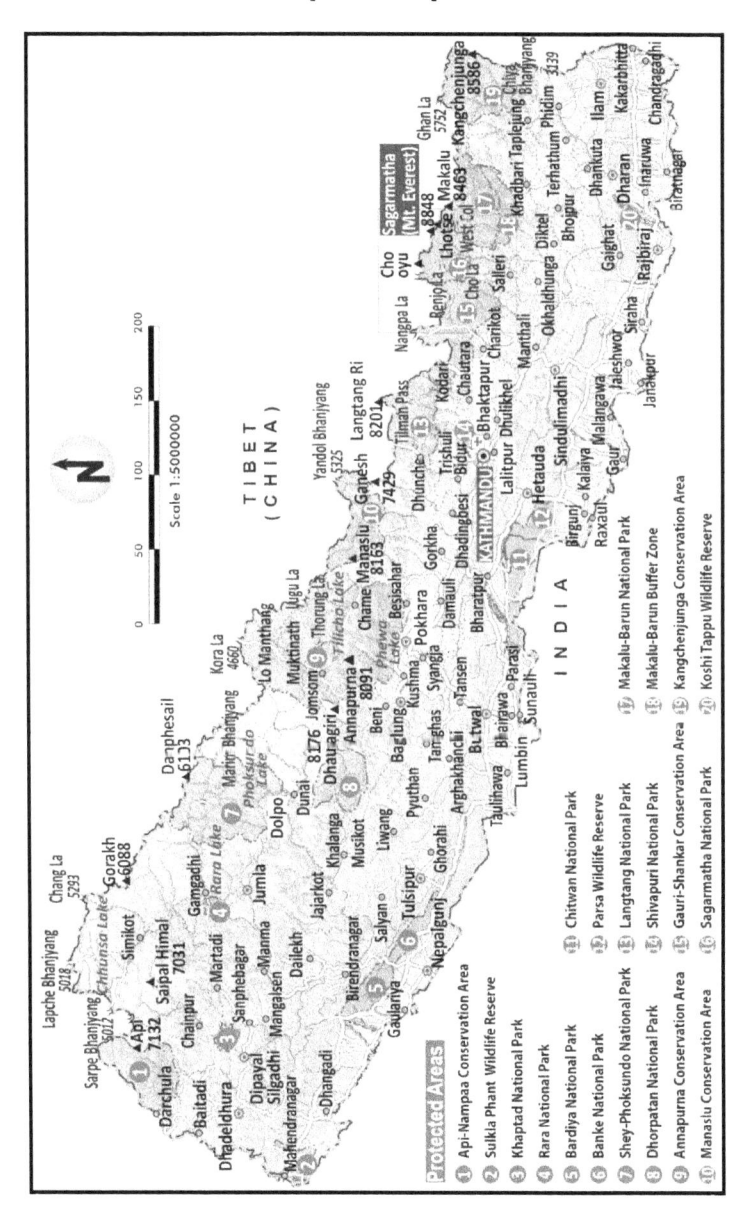

Map of Thamel

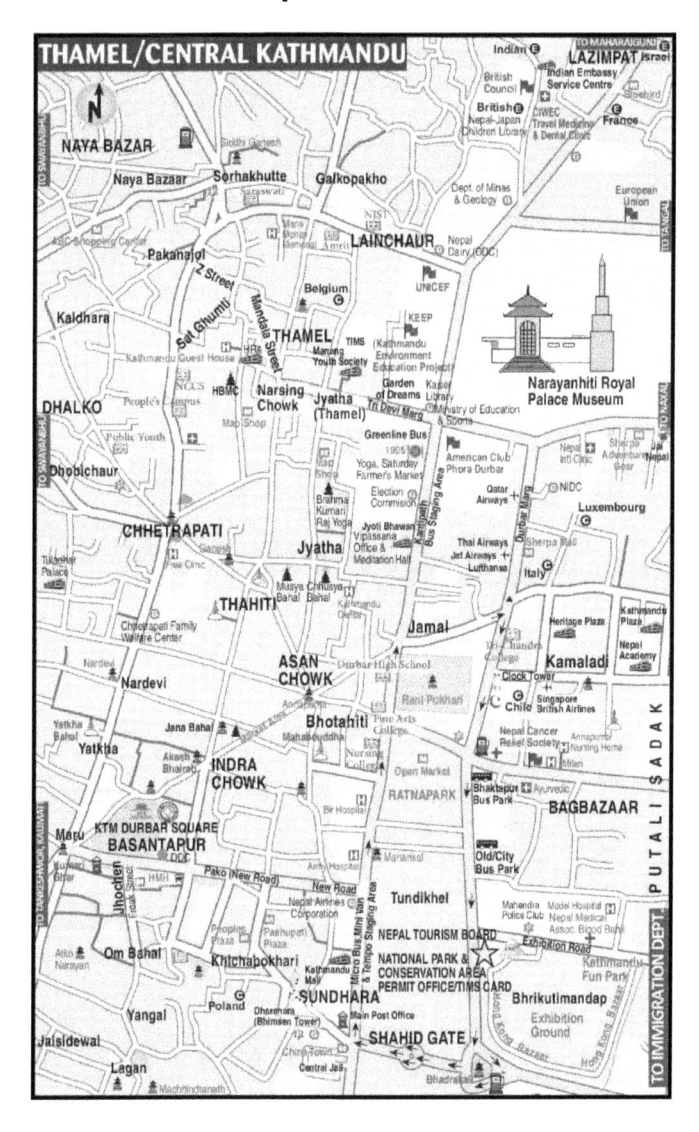

Map of Central Kathmandu

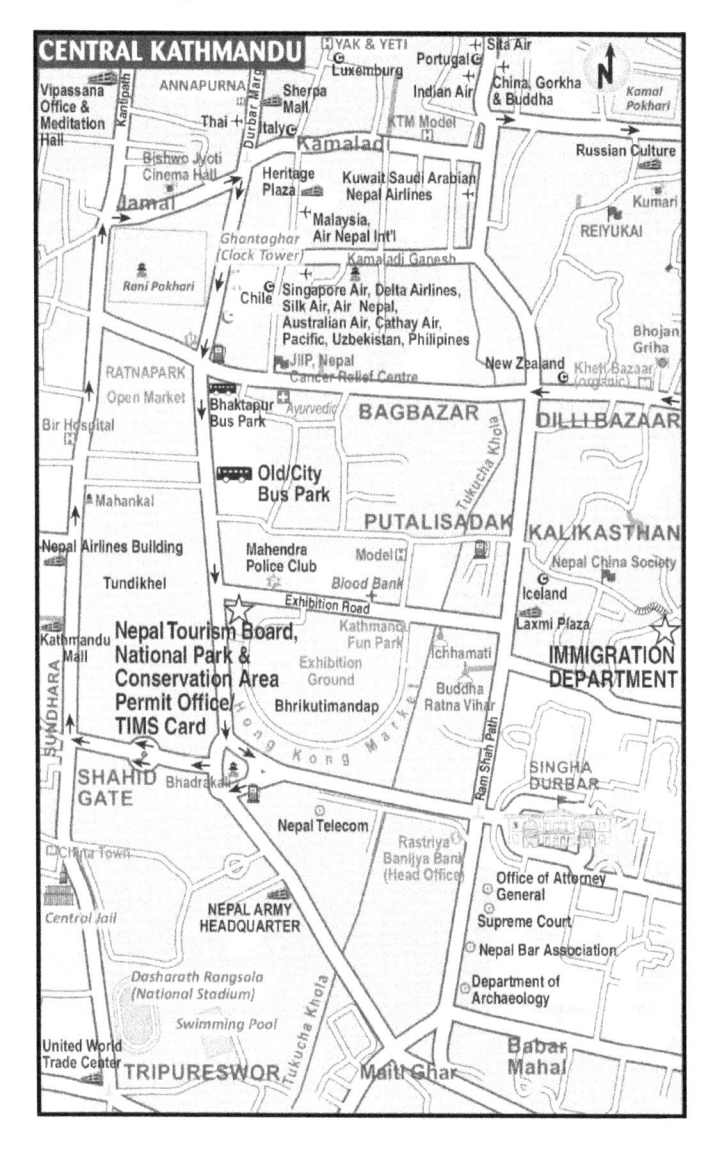

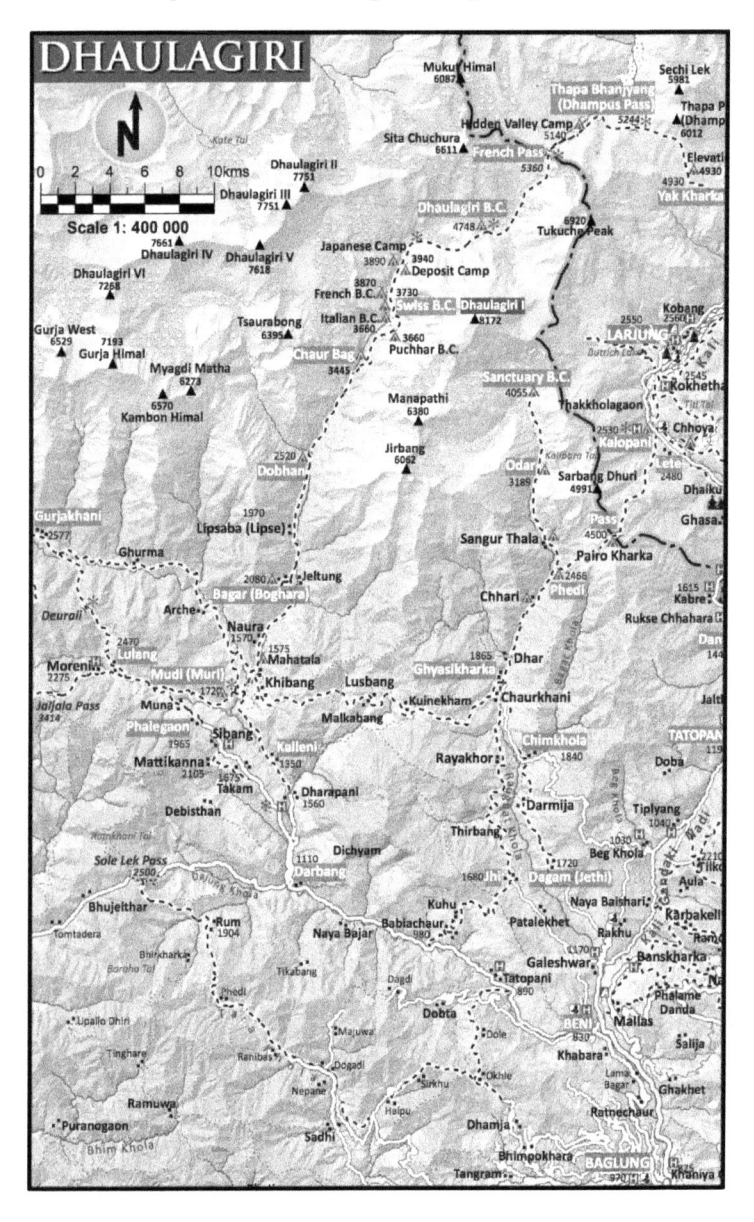

Map of Dhaulagiri region West

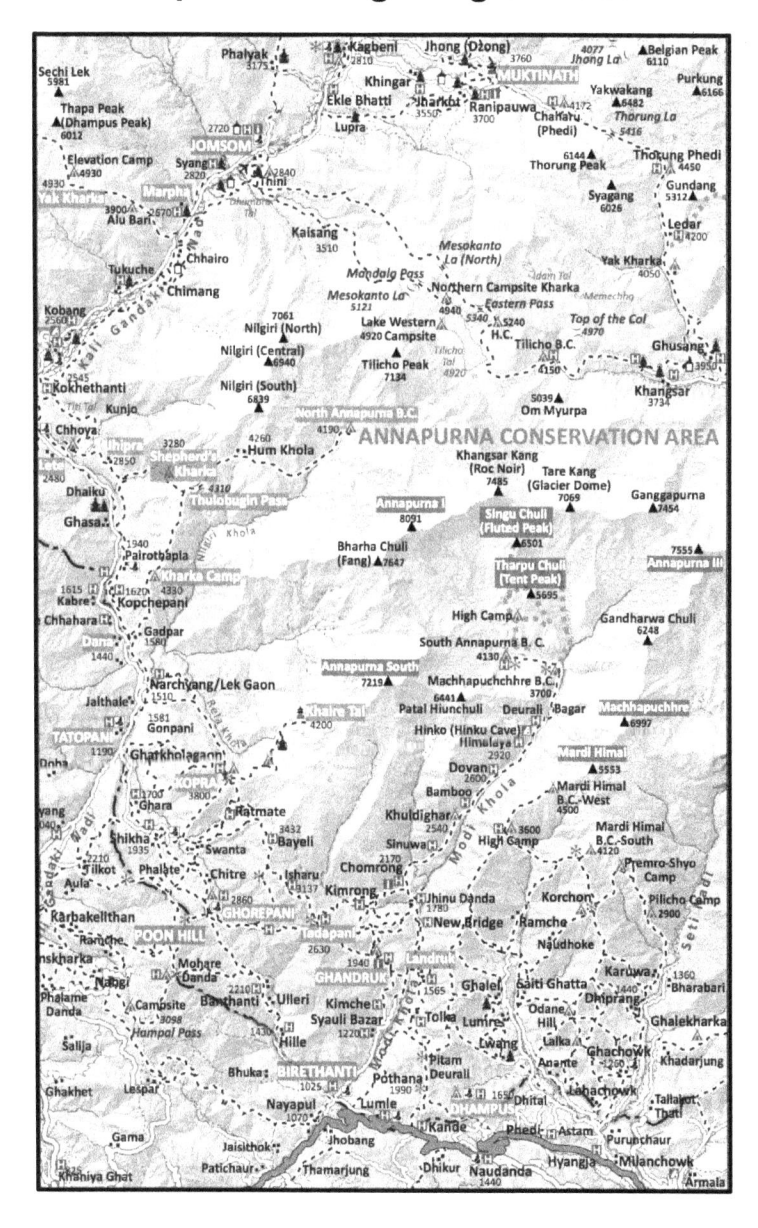

Map of Dhaulagiri region East

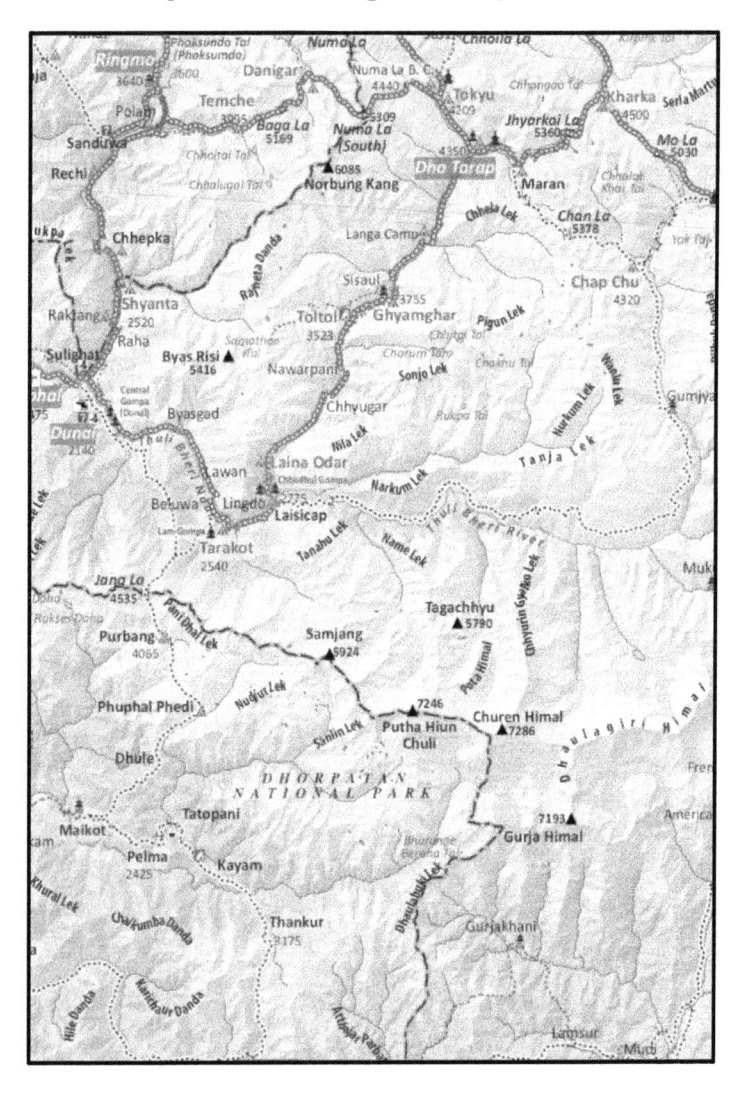

Map of Dhaulagiri–Dolpo West

Map of Dhaulagiri–Dolpo East

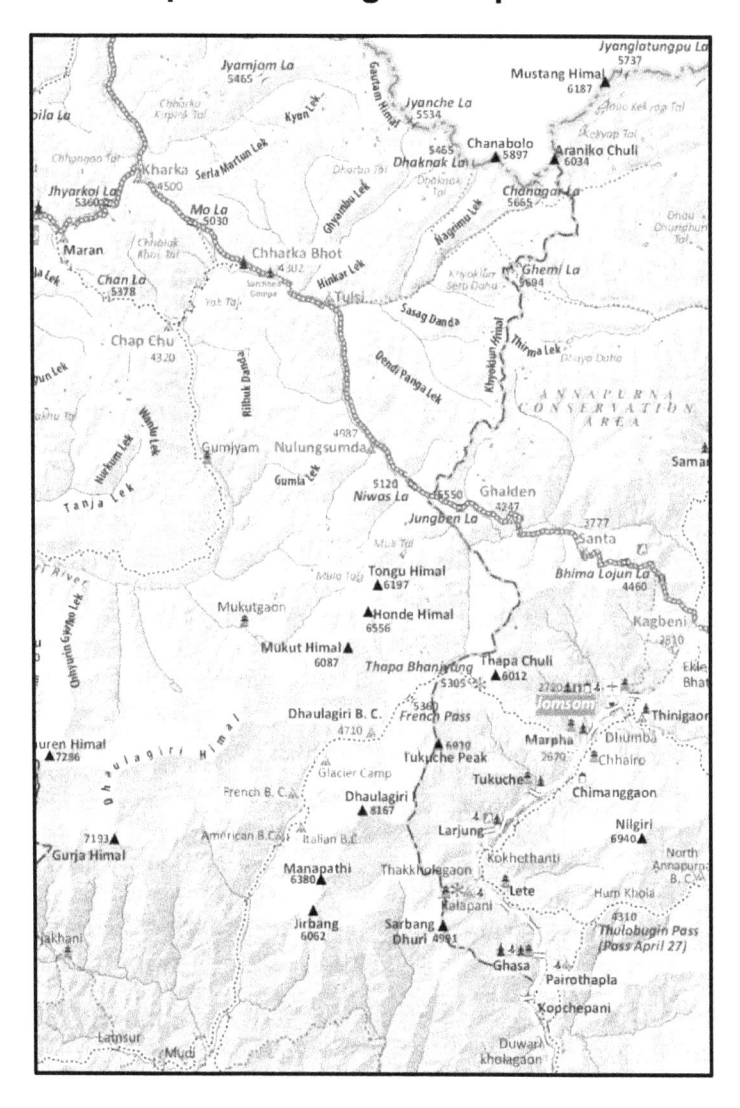

About the authors

Siân Pritchard-Jones and Bob Gibbons met in 1983, on a trek from Kashmir to Ladakh. By then Bob had already driven an ancient Land Rover from England to Kathmandu (in 1974), and overland trucks across Asia, Africa and South America. He had also lived in Kathmandu for two years, employed as a trekking company manager. Before they met, Siân worked in computer programming and systems analysis.

Since they met they have been leading and organising treks in the Alps, Nepal and the Sahara, as well as driving a bus overland to Nepal. Journeys by a less ancient (only 31-year-old) Land Rover from England to South Africa provided the basis for several editions of the Bradt guide **Africa Overland**, including the sixth edition published in April 2014.

In 2007 they wrote the Cicerone guide to **Mount Kailash** and Western Tibet, as well updating the **Grand Canyon** guide. Their **Annapurna** trekking guide was first published by Cicerone in January 2013, with the second edition in early 2017.

In 2015 they were in Nepal during the earthquakes and published **Earthquake Diaries: Nepal 2015**. A Pictorial Guide to the **Horn of Africa** (Djibouti, Eritrea, Ethiopia and Somaliland), **Australia: Red Centre Treks** and **In Search of the Green-Eyed Yellow Idol**, a 40-year travelogue & autobiography, are all published by Expedition World/CreateSpace/Amazon.

Kanchi's Tale is a new series of books covering various expeditions as seen through the eyes of a young Nepalese mountain dog – an educational doggie travelogue!

For Himalayan Map House they are writing a new series of trekking guidebooks: **Himalayan Travel Guides**. See next page for titles so far published. All books are also available on Amazon websites worldwide.

Magical view of Dhaulagiri South Face

Other books by the authors

Bradt (*www.bradtguides.com***)**
Africa Overland --- 2005, 2009, 2014

Cicerone (*www.cicerone.co.uk***)**
The **Mount Kailash** Trek --- 2007
Annapurna: A Trekker's Guide --- 2013, 2017

CreateSpace/Amazon (*www.amazon.com***)**
All HMH titles below
Ladakh: A Land of Magical Monasteries --- 2014
In Search of the Green-Eyed Yellow Idol --- 2015, 2016
(an autobiography)
Earthquake Diaries: Nepal 2015 --- 2015
The Horn of Africa --- 2016
Australia: Red Centre Treks --- 2016
Kanchi's Tale:
Kanchi goes to Makalu Base Camp --- 2017
Kanchi goes to the Tibesti, Chad --- 2017
Chad: Tibesti, Ennedi & Borkou --- 2017
Karakoram: The Highway of History --- 2018

Himalayan Map House (HMH)
(*www.himalayanmaphouse.com*)
Himalayan Travel Guides (HTG)
(*www.himalayantravelguides.com*)
& Amazon worldwide (*www.amazon.com***)**

Manaslu & Tsum Valley --- 2013, 2016, 2019; **Dolpo** --- 2014
Ganesh Himal --- 2014; **Langtang** --- 2014, 2018
Everest --- 2014, 2018; **Rolwaling** --- 2015
Mustang --- 2016; **Kanchenjunga** --- 2017
Makalu --- 2017; **West Nepal** --- 2017
Dhaulagiri --- 2018; **Nepal Himalaya** --- 2015, 2017

Pilgrims (*www.pilgrimsonlineshop.com***)**
Kathmandu: Valley of the Green-Eyed Yellow Idol --- 2005
Ladakh: Land of Magical Monasteries --- 2006
Kailash & Guge: Land of the Tantric Mountain --- 2006